Library of
Davidson College

Drugs, Parents, and Children

Drugs, Parents, and Children

The Three-Way Connection

By Mitchell S. Rosenthal, M.D.
and Ira Mothner

1972
Houghton Mifflin Company Boston

First Printing c

Copyright © 1972 by Mitchell S. Rosenthal and Ira Mothner
All rights reserved. No part of this work may be reproduced
or transmitted in any form by any means, electronic or
mechanical, including photocopying and recording, or by
any information storage or retrieval system, without
permission in writing from the publisher.
ISBN: 0-395-12718-1
Library of Congress Catalog Card Number: 73-162010
Printed in the United States of America

For all the boys and girls who made it back

Contents

Introduction ix

PART ONE

1. Society's Children Are Your Kids 3
2. The Prevalence of Druggism 15
3. More Vulnerable Than Others 23
4. Starting Out Straight 33
5. The Adolescent Storm 45
6. Dealing with Drugs 53
7. The Phoenix Way 77

PART TWO

8. The Adamses 101
9. The Browns 122
10. The Cowans 141
11. A Few Final Words 172

Index 175

Introduction

THIS BOOK IS FOR PARENTS and *about* parents, as well as about drugs and children. It is a guide to understanding what is probably the most disquieting dilemma of our times: the number of young people who have turned to drugs to help them solve or avoid the problems of living.

In a frenzy of concern, some parents and some communities demand solutions the same size as the problem, huge answers. They want vast educational campaigns for drug prevention, massive treatment programs, and rigid enforcement of drug prohibitions to cut off drugs at or near the source. They demand all this from the same professionals, politicians, and policemen who have repeatedly failed to control drugs in the past and are no better prepared to do so now.

There are many plans proposed today to end rampaging drug abuse, and few of them assign much responsibility to the family. Conventional wisdom seems to have relegated the family to the sociological scrap heap, dumped it as an outdated and underpowered piece of social machinery. The search is for institutional answers that are political, programmable, and easily evaluated.

But even though the failures of our institutions contribute heavily to it, drug abuse is not an institutional problem. It is a human problem that will only be solved in human terms. The family remains the best bulwark against drugs. But parents can't go it alone — communities will have to provide parents the means to meet the needs of their drug-troubled young.

We have written this book to help parents understand what they are up against, what they can do, and how they can do it. Drugs do not exist apart from other community problems; neither can they be separated from other aspects of family life. To deal with drugs, parents must first deal with their children and with each other. To help youngsters face their inevitable encounter with drugs, many parents will need to establish more intense relationships with them. Parents, working together to reach out and keep in touch with their children, may discover new ways of understanding and valuing each other.

Part One

Part One

1. Society's Children Are Your Kids

DRUGS ARE DANGEROUS, and parents protect children from danger. They stop their youngsters from stepping out into traffic. They don't wait until the children are old enough to recognize the risks for themselves. They pull infants back from window ledges, steep stairs, and the water's edge, because these are obvious perils. Drugs are an obvious peril too, and the best protection young people have against this particular peril is their parents. Most of the time, parents can prevent their children from using drugs — or stop them if they have already begun.

Yet a great number of parents have come to believe that drugs are strangely different from other dangers. They have heard that drugs are everybody's problem (and by implication nobody's in particular), or society's problem that society must attend to. Too many of them have happily swallowed the notion that they are somehow incapable of dealing with their own children's drug troubles. It is a responsibility they shed with relief, for drugs frighten parents. Drugs are mysterious, and they feel ill equipped to cope with them, unwilling to trust the things they do know, anxious to avoid the shame or guilt that is most often the initial parental response to drug problems.

Rather than face the troubles at home, some parents look beyond their families at the impact of drugs on the community. This is indeed everybody's problem, and the hard truth is that we do not yet have satisfactory ways of controlling rampaging drug abuse. Drugs are laced into the whole tangle of social stresses that make up the frustrating reality of our times. We cannot solve all our problems cheaply, easily, or right now. We do not know as much as we need to know about the persistence of poverty, why some children learn more readily than others, or how to hang on to environmental basics like clean air and water. But the absence of wholesale solutions does not prevent us from working out single, individual ones. It is not necessary to raise the reading level of the nation's entire sixth grade population before we can raise that of an individual child. Nor does our inability to cope with drugs as a community dilemma prevent individual families from solving their own drug problems (at least those families capable of problem solving). If anything, the community dilemma has been created in part by the failure of so many families to do just that.

Most parents are truly unprepared to get on with the job of dealing with drugs. They just don't know enough, and what they do know is a bizarre tangle of vintage myths and new magical promises. Until fairly recently, most of the information parents received came from policemen. Its purpose was not to inform but to scare the citizenry, and it was loaded with half-truths and untruths. The Federal Bureau of Narcotics encouraged the notion of "drug-crazed addicts," which was picked up and spun into fantasies the whole nation believed.

These lurid tales went out of style sometime after World War II and were replaced by another, somewhat more realistic fiction — "the drug slave." While Nelson Algren's novel *The Man with the Golden Arm* focused on the realities of addiction, the books, plays, and films that followed it gave rise to a widely held and completely unwarranted belief in the horrors of withdrawal. With this came faith in a kind of inescapable drug doom, the conviction that addiction is instant and permanent — one shot and the junkie is hooked for life, even one puff of marijuana and the innocent user is forever lost.

It didn't much matter what parents chose to believe about

drugs when there were few drug users around and no drug crisis. But they can hardly stand by these fantasies or even lesser ones when their children are bringing home a street knowledge — often incomplete and sometimes fatally misleading — that is miles closer to the truth.

Today, the misuse of drugs is pandemic. In New York City, it is the chief cause of death among young people fifteen to thirty. Heroin broke out of the ghetto years back and has moved into better neighborhoods and on to the suburbs. The newer addicts are younger, whiter, and more middle-class, and more of them are girls. New York was home to about 150,000 addicts at the end of 1971, while estimates of the national addict population range from less than a quarter to more than half a million.

But the increase in heroin addiction is small compared with the gains scored by other psychoactive drugs. Misuse of nonnarcotic psychoactive or mind-changing drugs has ballooned grotesquely during the past five years. And the great consumers, the new misusers, are getting younger and younger. While the median age for starting with drugs is now seventeen, that median may well drop to sixteen or fifteen if the current trend continues. High school principals in areas as far removed from traditional hard-drug country as rural New Hampshire and Idaho estimate that as many as half of their students have used marijuana, that 20 percent smoke it with fair frequency. A 1970 study in one California school district found that more than one third of the students had smoked marijuana at some time and close to one quarter were regular users. The number of regular users had not increased since a 1968 survey was made of the same schools (when similar results were reported by studies in other California suburbs). However, the number of youngsters with LSD experience had doubled by 1970 to more than 10 percent. Meanwhile, a study of students attending several branches of the State University of New York showed that the number of younger people already using drugs by the time they reached college had moved up sharply, and that five times

6   Drugs, Parents, and Children

as many undergraduates were using drugs in 1969 than in 1965. What these numbers mean is that there is close to an even chance that your youngsters will play around with some drug, someday. It is the worst kind of unreality to expect them to scamper through adolescence without ever coming up against drugs. Since you can't protect your children from what has become an almost inevitable encounter, you had best prepare them for it and prepare yourself, too.

What you are arming against, what has hit American families in the last few years, is an epidemic of *druggism, the habitual use of a psychoactive drug as a means of dealing with or avoiding reality.* There are plenty of kids now lost on drugs who will never be, by any accurate definition of the word, addicts. This does not mean they are not and will not remain sick. Any kind of druggism is a true disease, just as real and just as destructive as alcoholism or addiction, its most easily recognizable forms.

Yet druggism is not so different from any other destructive avenue up which young people sometimes venture. When youngsters take off, heading straight for trouble, there is usually a reason for it. But they may start to act out — to set off on self-destructive routes for reasons that have little to do with their homes or parents. Parents can prevent children from harming themselves most of the time. Yet they can't do this when young people choose to harm themselves in ways their parents are unprepared to prevent.

You can usually close off druggism as a route your youngsters will take by starting to work early on their attitudes, teaching them and showing them healthy and responsible ways of behaving. You must deal with their feelings too, keeping the channels clear so that you can hear when they are troubled or pressured. Doing this effectively may mean working on your own feelings and attitudes and developing a reasonable and knowledgeable position on drugs.

If drugs troubles come, you must be ready to stick by your attitude and make your attitude stick. You cannot wait for druggism to "burn out." You cannot wait for your youngster to wise up, any more than you can wait for a three-year-old to learn about traffic. Your attitude about drugs is no attitude at all if it permits children to decide about drugs for themselves; it will not be responsible if it allows adolescents to use psychoactive drugs regularly or even occasionally. To many modern parents, a blanket drug prohibition sounds hard-nosed and autocratic. It is. But there are sound reasons for it and ways to establish it and make it hold. Parents have more muscle than they are usually prepared to use, more resources than they are willing to put into play. All that is required is one simple but very difficult decision — making up your mind to go the limits necessary to keep your youngster clean.

Before you can make that decision or even put together an attitude about drugs, you are probably going to need more information than you now have. Most parents first want to know about drugs themselves, and these are the questions they most often ask.

What are psychoactive drugs?

A drug is any chemical substance that affects living protoplasm (just about anything that can be sniffed, swallowed, shot, smoked, or rubbed into the skin). A psychoactive drug is one that works on the mind, alters consciousness. Alcohol is a psychoactive drug; so is marijuana. But the kinds of substances youngsters use to turn themselves on or off is nearly limitless. They'll use nutmeg, cleaning fluid, or morning-glory seeds. Kids have tried and died on aerosol propellant and glue. A few years back, there was a run on banana-peel scrapings when the silly word spread that, dried and smoked, they would work almost as well as marijuana.

What is addiction?

Most psychoactive drugs cannot properly be called addictive.

8   *Drugs, Parents, and Children*

Addiction is caused by the misuse of narcotics (opium and opium products like codeine, morphine, and heroin), synthetic narcotics (like methadone), and barbiturates.

The addiction process is automatic and easy to observe, describe, and predict, and for many years it was the only aspect of drug abuse that anybody understood. Narcotic users develop a tolerance for their drug, so that they require larger and larger doses to achieve the same effect. If the purpose is to relieve pain, a doctor must increase the dosage to keep pace with his patient's tolerance. Narcotic abusers must have progressively heavier doses to get their high, the feeling of well-being that peaks at a point of absolute euphoria.

As his tolerance builds, the narcotic user begins to *require* the drug. Without it, he feels real pain and starts into withdrawal, his body's way of protesting this sudden deprivation. What causes all the fuss during withdrawal is the autonomic nervous system, the network that attends to such bodily functions as breathing and digestion and over which one has very little control. When the body is denied the drug it has grown accustomed to, the autonomic system starts sending out confused signals, bombarding its outposts with garbled messages. The result is to turn everything "on." The addict in withdrawal feels a general malaise, suffers nausea, diarrhea, a runny nose, headaches.

Does fear of withdrawal keep most addicts hooked?

Most long-term addicts have gone through withdrawal several times. They withdraw in jail when they are arrested. They often commit themselves to detoxification clinics (for medically assisted withdrawal) to bring their habits down to a manageable size when they have trouble finding money to feed them.

Withdrawal is fairly short-lived and not nearly as severe as "realistic" fiction or even some naive medical observation would lead one to believe. The period of acute discomfort rarely lasts longer than thirty-six hours or is more unpleasant than a bad bout of flu (which also plays havoc with the autonomic system). However, withdrawal is an obliging syndrome that usually meets the expectations of both observers and addicts. Addicts with really heavy habits do have a rougher time, and it goes harder for those in areas where heroin comes in a stronger mix. (Most street heroin is combined with quinine or milk sugar and is rarely more than 10 percent pure.)

Are addicts dangerous?

Addicts are not vicious people, and heroin itself does not make them vicious. Most addicts are in fact frightened people, but their fear doesn't stop them from committing crimes, sometimes violent crimes.

Because addiction is a costly business and few addicts can afford a heavy habit (fewer still can hold down a job that pays enough to meet their growing drug needs), addict crime seems a simple matter of cause and effect. But the effect is often present before the cause. Many addicts steal before they use drugs. Stealing is a parallel activity; it provides the same kind of excitement, the same self-destructive possibilities that drug taking provides. A British study of addicts who received prescriptions for heroin from clinics in London noted that more than half had been convicted of some criminal offense not connected with drugs even before they began using heroin. Even when provided with prescriptions for low-cost drugs, more than one-third of these addicts continued to support themselves wholly or partly by criminal activity.

With the high cost of illicit drugs in the United States, a hundred-dollar-a-day habit is not uncommon. An addict with a habit that size has got to come up with that much money every day, seven days a week. Unless he obtains it legally or trades drugs to earn it, he must rob it in cash or steal enough TV sets, hi-fis, cameras, clocks, radios, fur coats, suits, furniture, industrial equipment, roast beefs, canned goods, or jewelry to net that much after fencing or peddling on the street. The recent landslide of big-city crime, the terrifying number of robberies, burglaries, purse snatches, and other larcenies has been blamed on the equally dramatic increase in heroin addiction, and there is every reason to believe this equation is an accurate one.

When politicians today claim concern about drugs, they are not worrying about the victims of addiction, but the victims of addicts, the people who get robbed. While this is a legitimate concern, it means most of the public noise, the sounds that come from city halls and state capitols, does not reflect any real commitment to ending druggism or even addiction. The public wants crime under control and junkies off the streets; whether they are shot or cured does not bother the average citizen.

Does smoking marijuana lead to heroin addiction?

Most young people who misuse drugs are not going to become addicts. Some will, for every heroin user must start somewhere, usually with marijuana or pills. By far the largest number of youngsters who try grass or even pop a few amphetamine spansules will never develop any kind of a habit. They will try drugs a few times, then drop them. Others, who don't quit early in the game — while it is still a game — can become habituated to or dependent upon whatever drug they have chosen. Unless it is a narcotic, they won't become addicts, but drugs will be a necessary and constant part of their lives. The nonaddicting psychoactives can sometimes be even more damaging, more destructive than narcotics.

What are the drugs youngsters most commonly misuse?

When youngsters turn on, they are moving their heads in one of three directions — up, down, or out. That is, they are using drugs that stimulate, depress, or distort.

Among stimulants, the best-known and most often used are the amphetamines (speed, pep pills). They can keep you awake if you're sleepy or get you through a double shift or an extra night's work. Not only will they ward off sleep, but taken regularly, they will cut your appetite. They are heavily prescribed for dieters.

Although amphetamines mask these needs, the body still requires food and rest. The adolescent body needs lots of both, and the youngster on amphetamines soon starts to run down. His body can't take the strain. Meanwhile, his head is having a high time, for the drug creates an illusion of strength and power and produces a kind of euphoria. When pills no longer seem to work, no longer can conceal the need for rest, some youngsters inject amphetamine. As with other drugs that are shot, there is a "rush" that comes with injection, an instant sexual flash. However, after the effects of the drug subside, the user hits a depressive depth so terrifying that he often shoots more amphetamine to get back to normal. The result is a "speed binge" that may last for several days.

Amphetamines can produce in some users what the AMA drug committee describes as "an acute and florid paranoid psychosis," including unpredictable violence, and the word on the street is that "speed kills."

A few years back, it would have been unnecessary to mention cocaine. It wasn't common. Legally a narcotic (listing it that way made for a neater law), cocaine is actually a stimulant. More and more of it is showing up in the inventories of dealers who once traded only in heroin. It is expensive, and still fairly hard to come by, and only adolescents with sophisticated tastes will be using it.

Youngsters don't usually restrict themselves to a single drug, once they have gone past smoking marijuana. They experiment, try different combinations and as many kinds of psychoactives as they can find and dare use. If they go up with stimulants, the chances are they also come down with depressants, and there are all kinds of depressants. Alcohol is a depressant, narcotics are depressants, and so are tranquilizers. But barbiturates are the depressants most young people will start with. They are common and easy to come by; more than four hundred tons are made in a year and commonly prescribed as sleeping pills or to calm jittery patients. They are addicting — although there is a limit to anyone's tolerance, and more than three thousand users die from overdoses each year. Some of these ODs are preplanned, for suicide is another way — the ultimately self-destructive way — that adolescents act out their rage or despair.

For most middle-class youngsters, the drugs of choice are psychedelics. There is romance, a tradition, and a mystery about these "mind-expanding" substances. In other cultures and at other times, they have been the socially sanctioned routes to greater spirituality or understanding. As a result, they have great attraction for bright young people, even fairly healthy ones. Marijuana is a psychedelic drug, a mild one. Leaves of the female Indian hemp plant are dried and crushed to make marijuana, while hashish comes from the concentrated resin of these leaves.

Marijuana does relax the user and brings a gentle kind of euphoria. There is some distortion of the senses (time and distance are hard to measure), and even mild hallucinations are experienced from time to time. These sensory distortions are greater with hashish and increase as the user moves up the psychedelic potency scale to peyote (made from certain cactus buttons), mescaline (refined from peyote), and LSD (lysergic acid diethylamide). There are other hallucinogens, and in varying degrees they all produce visual images, sharpen or seem to sharpen the senses so users hear, feel, taste, and even smell with uncanny sensitivity. The more potent psychedelics are literally mind-bending drugs. They shift or change the mental set of the user, and this mind-bending can take some tragic turns. Bad trips, in which anxieties get out of control, are frequent, and can produce psychotic episodes. Bluntly, this means a young user may come off a bad trip truly out of his mind, dangerous to himself and everyone else.

How can I tell what drug my child is using?

You can't. Experienced observers can spot a youngster who is feeling the effects of a drug, but it isn't easy to tell just what the child has taken.

In one experiment, groups of drug users were asked to judge which of their number had been given stimulants, which tranquilizers, and which had taken placebos (pills that had no effect at all). They were wrong as often as they were right and were no more accurate about what they themselves had taken; nor did psychiatrists who viewed films of the experimental groups have any better luck picking out who had taken what drug.

Parents should be looking for general indications that something is wrong with their child, not specific symptoms of drug misuse. If a youngster suddenly does badly in school, becomes sloppy, or loses a great deal of weight; if his complexion has changed, or his eyes are red and bagged most of the time — these are clues that something is amiss. It may not be drugs, but it is something the parents should be concerned about.

When your youngster comes home drunk, it doesn't much matter whether he has been drinking beer or bourbon. Nor should his choice of drugs matter much. Yet parents will try to make distinctions between drugs, deciding some are safer than others, while in reality there is little difference. The habitual use of *any* drug is druggism, and therefore destructive. Debating the virtues of various psychoactives with drug-using youngsters is playing their game, allowing them to duck the real issues.

How harmful are the nonaddicting psychoactives?

We don't know as much as we want to know about the physical dangers of psychoactive drugs. There is some evidence that amphetamines can harm the liver and cause chronic brain disorders. Heavily sedated patients in mental hospitals develop

14 Drugs, Parents, and Children

an ailment called tardive dyskinesia and have difficulty controlling their speech and facial muscles or even maintaining normal posture. Youngsters who inject their drugs are vulnerable to hepatitis, abcesses, and collapsed veins. However, the theory that chromosomes broken down by LSD do not repair themselves (which would push up the odds against users' having normal children) has not been confirmed.

The great concern of many parents about the possible physical dangers of psychoactive drugs is misplaced. Tobacco, alcohol, and even too many ice-cream cones are more physically dangerous than many psychoactive drugs. These drugs act where they are supposed to act — in the mind, and that is where the damage is done. While psychological hazards include the psychoses produced by amphetamines and LSD, there are far more common results of druggism. Youngsters who are regularly using drugs become muddle-headed and vague, lose interest in school, become depressed, anxious, and sometimes hostile. They can suffer profound despair. Drugs offer an illusory security from adolescent anxieties, but the young people who seek security from drugs actually thwart the adolescent process. They have chosen drugs instead of growing up and, if they persist in that choice, they will *not* grow up.

2. The Prevalence of Druggism

WE TAKE A KIND OF perverse pride in just how far things have come apart in our time. Nothing, we feel, was ever as big or as bad as it is today, and nowhere is it worse than here. Apparently we draw some comfort from the idea that our problems are unique. Druggism is not unique, and it is not new. Psychoactive drugs have long been used by sizable chunks of the population in countries all over the world.

Andean Indians know that chewing coca leaves makes it possible for them to work more easily at high altitudes. The cocaine extracted in this way gives them the same kind of lift Australian aborigines get from pituri leaves, while kat provides a mild buzz for most workers on the Arabian Peninsula.

When the British ruled India, they asked the same kinds of questions about marijuana that a number of American parents are asking today. To answer them, the British set up the Indian Hemp Drug Commission, which conducted an exhaustive study of marijuana use. After almost two years, the commission concluded that there was no evidence of mental, moral, or physical disability caused by moderate use of the drug. "Moderation," reads their 1894 report, "does not lead to excess in hemp any more than it does in alcohol. Regular, moderate use of ganja or bhang produced the same effect as moderate and regular doses of whiskey. Excess is confined to the idle and dissipated." When the commissioners found no good reason to prohibit use of the drug (and it is doubtful that the British could have enforced such a ban), they next considered taxing marijuana. However, an Indian colleague dissuaded them from this course by arguing that both Hindu custom and Muslim law prohibited taxing anything that gave pleasure to the poor.

There has always been tolerance, in most of the world, for the excesses of the poor. A kind of guilty class-consciousness permitted the most deprived citizens to drug themselves. The British hemp commissioners recognized that marijuana would probably be abused to the same extent that alcohol was. Considering the amount of alcoholism in England during the first part of the century then ending, the commissioners were leaving plenty of leeway.

"The social and hygienic conditions under which a great part of the working classes in the Far East live are of so low a standard that these classes of people strive to find some form of diversion permitting them to forget for at least some moments the hardships of life." So reads a 1930 League of Nations report on opium use. To be fair, the authors believed that, "In the Far East generally and especially in tropical countries, where the population often suffers from dysentery, typhoid, malaria and other fevers, there is a widespread belief that opium taken habitually, whether eaten or smoked, will act as a prophylactic against such diseases and cure them."

Opium has been widely used at various times, and entire labor forces in some areas have been known to depend upon it. By masking symptoms and soothing discomfort, opium can get workers through a hard day in tropical mines and factories, workers who would otherwise be in too much pain to leave their beds. It is difficult, however, to assess how much of the pain relieved by the drug is also caused by it.

The Chinese spotted opium as a troublemaker and banned the drug in 1729. Later, British merchants, greedy for Chinese tea, objected to this ban. They wanted to trade Indian-grown opium for the tea, and it took two Opium Wars, in 1842 and 1858, to overcome Chinese resistance to this scheme.

When Chinese laborers came to the United States, they

brought along their pipes and opium. By that time, both paregoric and laudanum, solutions of the opium poppy, were already common remedies in both Europe and the United States. In 1830, a German pharmacist refined the active alkaloid of opium — morphine. The hypodermic syringe was invented twenty-three years later and physicians, seeking some way to cure morphism (as addiction to morphine was called), tried injecting the drug under the skin. It didn't work; morphism only increased. In Europe, wounded veterans of the Crimean War (1854–1856) and the Franco-Prussian War (1870–1871) brought their habits home from the battlefields. In the United States, thousands of morphine addicts from the Civil War carried what became known as "the army disease" across the country.

Toward the end of the nineteenth century, a great many Americans were hooked, mostly on patent medicines laced with opium, which were widely dispensed without prescriptions. We have only crude estimates of the actual numbers, but we can assume that there were a good many more addicts then than there are today. Most of them were women who kept an opium-spiked tonic on hand for what was politely termed "female trouble" and found themselves nipping it with fair frequency.

At the start of this century, the national mood was puritanical. Temperance advocates were preparing to push through a national Prohibition Amendment, and the ranks of the godly were closing in on drugs, too. San Francisco had passed an anti-opium ordinance in 1875 (aimed at Asian immigrants whose "opium dens" were a handy target for those who yelled "yellow peril" and worried about cheap Chinese labor). By 1903, several states had narcotics laws on their books, and President Theodore Roosevelt proposed the first international meeting on opium, held in Shanghai in 1909. Three years later, at The Hague, the International Opium Convention was signed, and each participating nation pledged to control traffic in the drug, suppress smoking, and restrict opium to medical use.

Keeping its part of the opium pact, the United States adopted the Harrison Act in 1914. Legitimate traffic in opium dropped to a medical minimum. Illegal traffic began, not only in opium and morphine, but in acetylated morphine, developed in 1898 as a cure for addiction and named — because of its heroic mission — heroin.

The number of addicts in the nation did drop markedly after the Harrison Act was passed. At first, medical help was easy for addicts to obtain. Doctors would prescribe morphine for them, and a number of addiction clinics were started. But in 1919 the Narcotics Division of the Treasury Department (then responsible for administering the Harrison Act) began taking doctors to court, charging they had no right to prescribe opium for addicts, even to ease withdrawal. With the Behrman decision in 1922, the Supreme Court supported the Narcotics Division's stand. The high court backed away from that hard-line verdict three years later, but it was too late. Now wary of harassment by narcotics agents, doctors avoided the risky business of treating addicts.

In time, some nonaddictive drugs were also proscribed. Congress was stampeded by the Bureau of Narcotics (with threats of drug-crazed youths committing violence in the streets) into passing the Marijuana Tax Act of 1937. Although the act failed a recent Supreme Court test and the current federal drug laws reflect a more realistic understanding of drug abuse, our national policy remains essentially punitive. We have attempted to protect ourselves from drug dangers by raising an imposing wall of law against them.

In so doing, we have doubled our dilemma. Making drug use a crime makes drug users criminals. Their druggism becomes not only a danger to their health and their heads, but also a threat to their physical security, their social well-being. Driving drug use underground, making it a furtive activity in defiance of the law, sets up a row of barriers for parents or communities that want to deal with dependency problems. They must first find them, ferret them out, and then overcome the social embarrassment of acknowledging that they exist. Many parents are so terrified of the legal implications of drug abuse that they would rather risk their youngsters' mental health than face the problem of their druggism.

The drug laws have made it difficult to get a proper handle on the issue of druggism, for druggism exists both within the law and outside it. There is a perfectly legal brand of druggism. Alcoholics do not break the law in their pursuit of alcohol. Nor do all those law-abiding types marching down to their corner pharmacies with legitimate prescriptions; their brand of drug dependency is medically sanctioned, and common.

We are concerned mostly with acute druggism among the young, and most of this is illegal. But we cannot ignore the chronic, legal kind of druggism favored by adults. The four-martini drinker is using a drug to deal with or avoid reality just as much as his pill-popping son is. The lady heavily into sleeping pills is at the same game, and so are a good many chubby housewives on amphetamine diet regimes.

Unwittingly, doctors have become the biggest pushers in the country, and drug companies will have a heavy reckoning to bear when they're called to account for all they have contributed to the spread of druggism. There is often little a doctor can do to make a patient better (for there is nothing physically wrong with almost two out of three visitors to his examining room). But doctors can always make their patients *feel* better, and too many see nothing wrong with doing just that. Henry L. Lennard and his co-authors put it best in *Mystification and Drug Misuse*: "Physicians and hippies alike tend to treat the body as if it were a machine and, paradoxically, to seek meaning through chemicals as well. Both are truly members of the same technological culture and both are enveloped by the same rapid demand for change." The doctor's narrow vision leads him to approach complex human situations like a body mechanic. "The logical extension of the enterprise of such 'technicians' is to develop and utilize tools," say Lennard and company.

"Drugs are tools that are introduced into human 'machines' to make them better or to make them run smoothly."

What is the point of all this drug taking? Often the patient is not being helped at all. Young doctors will prescribe a psychoactive drug because it makes *them*, the doctors, feel better, less powerless to effect some seemingly helpful change. Sometimes drugging benefits a third party or parties. In Omaha, Nebraska, between 5 and 10 percent of the city's 62,000 schoolchildren were recently being dosed with amphetamines and antidepressants on the advice of teachers who had labeled the youngsters either hyperactive or unmanageable. Because some institutionalized children, all severely disturbed, had been helped to control gross hyperactivity by the use of amphetamines, a local pediatrician proposed that the Omaha public schools undertake this wholesale program. The result was predictably messy, with kids swapping their pills in the schoolyards. Why were these children given drugs? Because drugs seemed a quick, easy way to cope with complex behavioral problems, or perhaps dispensing them was simpler than revising a stultifying curriculum.

The kindly family physician who solicitously sedates the bereaved widow is making things easier on her friends and family while denying her the full expression of her grief. Grief has an important function. To inhibit it works against what is actually best for the widow. Yet doctors frequently disregard the patient's needs when prescribing drugs. Handing out sedatives to hospital patients is not simply a matter of assuring a sound night's sleep for them all. It keeps them on the early-to-bed–early-to-rise schedule, the most convenient routine for the hospital.

While there are many situations in which psychoactive drugs are vital therapeutic tools, there are others in which they are not only unnecessary, but harmful. When drugs are used to control behavior in mental hospitals and some nursing homes, it cannot be argued that this treatment is always administered for the welfare of the patients. Sedated mental patients will frequently suffer debilitating side effects for no good reason. When older residents of nursing homes are heavily tranquilized, they are deprived of even the limited physical and social activity they can enjoy.

Doctors are pressured to prescribe psychoactives. They are encouraged by drug companies that push these products and by patients who demand them. The medical journals are gorged with artful inducements to hand out tranquilizers and antidepressants, not for specific ills, but at troublesome times. The makers of one tranquilizer suggest their product be prescribed for girls experiencing the normal stresses of starting college.

When a doctor gives psychoactive drugs to a patient who does not really need them, he is doing more than just choosing an easy way out for himself, for his patient, or for the patient's family. He is denying the patient the experience of working through and mastering a particular problem or situation. Avoiding the problem or situation is an undermining emotional experience that leaves the patient less able to deal with the next instance of emotional stress, the next personal crisis. The probability that the patient will continue to need drugs thus increases. By ignoring these consequences, the doctor is doing what every drug user does and opting for the quick and easy answer that is no answer at all.

Drugs are apparent short cuts to intimacy, self-knowledge, mystical experience, and bliss. The kids clutched together, passing around a joint, are often sharing only an illusion of intimacy. Since the drug provides this instant illusion, there is no need for the youngsters to give to one another, to work toward understanding each other, to try to share their thoughts and feelings. Most of us have experienced the false clarity of thought that comes after several drinks. The drug user reaches such a point quickly, and so begins to depend upon drugs to order his mind.

To come to grips with druggism, we have got to recognize that the way of drug use, the easy way, seems prevalent in our society, at least as that society is perceived by young people. Not every family consumes pills and nostrums to soothe and comfort, to relieve tensions and cure the "blahs." But what about the hours youngsters put in at television? An important part of their youth is spent watching the men in white coats hawk these remedies. The message is clear: "Drugs are necessary." They are necessary for the artificial good life lived by all those smiling people who are free from constipation, insomnia, and jumpy nerves. Those people are free from stress, too, since there are pills for that, for the overworked father and the frazzled mother. It isn't really necessary to grapple with human problems; there's a well-advertised way out. That is the message the kids are getting.

The fight against druggism starts early. It starts at home with the ways parents use or misuse drugs. But it goes deeper, down to the attitudes parents impart in the ordinary, everyday acts of being parents. Although the amount of information to which today's youngsters are exposed is much greater than the amounts any other generation has ever come up against, parents remain the basic source of knowledge for most young children. They support or refute whatever else the youngsters are learning. They can help to create a tolerance for the use of drugs as solutions to problems, or they can rule them out as a real alternative for their children.

3. More Vulnerable Than Others

EARLY IN THE CENTURY, before the psychoactive pharmacopoeia blossomed, drugs of abuse were most likely to be narcotics. Addiction then hit hardest a section of the population that was white, adult, rural, and as likely to be female as male. Most of these addicts had stumbled into druggism by mischance, hooked by opium-spiked nostrums or by heavy-handed doctoring at a time when and in places where medicine was more casually practiced than today, and before synthetic analgesics replaced the then widely used morphine. It isn't difficult to understand that kind of druggism.

Sometime after 1930, drugs came to town — not the best parts of town, but the black ghettos. They are still there, but no longer only there. Today, when most victims are young, neither a good address nor membership in the majority race can guarantee protection against drugs. There is much public wailing and moaning now that druggism has reached into the white middle class. This national concern was shamefully lacking when the drug-stricken were predominantly black, when the first wave of the present pandemic was cutting down ghetto young.

Just before the great drug boom, in 1964, when the omens were already fairly clear, an economist addressing the American Academy of Arts and Sciences came close to predicting what was in the offing. He wasn't worried about drugs but about the unemployment he assumed would result from greater automation. He claimed that we then faced such an explosive increase in leisure that within a mere ten years we might have to keep the unemployed portion of our population under sedation, unless we could quickly figure out something better for them to do.

The really unemployed portions of the population were, even then, getting a fair start on sedating themselves. Not that displaced industrial workers were hitting the needle or popping pills; they were out looking for work. But most of the unemployed blacks and unemployed young didn't even show up on the Labor Department tallies, because they weren't looking for work anymore. They had given up or settled for part-time jobs, casual jobs, or jobs that paid less than the legal or vital minimum.

Drug use among this group of unemployed, underemployed, and unemployable is not a matter of some devil finding work for idle hands (unless you take the militant black reading on it, that the white devil deals out the junk to keep black people down). It is the predictable result of whatever process (discrimination, credentialism, union power, automation) keeps large numbers of particular groups in a state of permanent or semipermanent dependency. They are the nonfunctional or minimally functional, the noncontributing or barely contributing members of our society, and they pay a heavy price for their enforced indolence. They punish themselves and try to punish us, both by taking drugs and by acting out in ways other than druggism, with criminality, violence, suicide, and the like.

They are vulnerable because they feel useless and immature, because they are often prevented from pulling their full load. Not only blacks, but all the minorities with undue representation in the economic underclass — Puerto Ricans, Indians, Chicanos — are all too frequently denied what are ordinary, everyday experiences for most people. Too many of them do not get up and go to work or go about their business, because they have no work to go to, no business to go about. Neither do the young, even the white middle-class young. But in their case there is a kind of time lock on the exclusion; if they wait a while they'll be included in. A third population, rarely lumped with the young and the black, also suffers from a noncontributory role in society — white middle-class women. Whether or not one sympathizes with the demands of the women's movement for a more participatory economy, the truth is that many women feel useless and insignificant and a large number of middle-class ladies are well into druggism, dependent mostly upon alcohol and legally acquired pills.

In the ghetto, where our present troubles began, the conditions that seem to encourage druggism also appear to erode the family's capacity to deal with it. What is actually eroded, in many cases, is the family itself. More than a million black people moved into central cities between 1960 and 1965. During the entire fifteen-year period ending in 1966, the black population of our twenty-five largest cities doubled. A great part of this migration started with the mechanization of Southern farms, which cost black families not only their jobs, but their homes as well. They went to the cities of the North and West, looking for work where work was available, but lacking the education and the skills needed to land those good jobs and finding many of the powerful unions standing in their way.

These were rural families, down home folk, used to the social controls of tightly knit communities, with a network of family and friends to help them through hard times and keep tabs on them, enforcing standards of behavior and decorum. Strangers in the big cities, they found few substitutes for this sense of community. The areas they moved into were already thick with crime and drugs. The old ways didn't hold up here, and there was nothing to replace them. The city itself lacked the capacity to enforce real social control. The most able, the natural community leadership, moved up and out, leaving behind the least able, criminals, addicts, and newcomers.

Youngsters found a street culture stronger and more vital than anything available at school or often at home. Traditional values were reversed on the street, with drug pushers and numbers kings the models of success. Many children formed an attitude about the law based upon rude encounters with white, lower-middle-class policemen, some of whom distrusted or even feared blacks. Police connivance at both the numbers racket and the drug trade did little to raise the law's esteem.

The ultimate peer group, the gang, replaced for many youngsters both family and community. While the gangs remained strong, many ghetto children were able to resist druggism. They stayed clean while they acted out in other ways, with violence and crime. There is some question now as to whether drugs destroyed the gangs or the police and youth workers were so successful cleaning them up and decriminalizing them that the gangs just fell apart and opened the way for drugs. Today, many of those same youth workers are back on the street, trying to knit the gangs together again.

Meanwhile, at home, the black family often found Father superfluous. There has long been a strong matriarchal tendency in black families, but it took the welfare system to actually drive Daddy out of the house. Unresponsive in many ways, the large industrial cities of the North and Midwest did provide a level of welfare assistance that was unavailable in the South. In most cities, that money wasn't paid while the family remained intact. Only when Father left were Mother and the children eligible for Aid to Families with Dependent Children. Even when the federal law was amended to allow unemployed fathers to remain at home, most states turned down that option, demanding that the old absent-father formula be retained.

After Father left home he often disappeared. Welfare investigators could force him to pay child support if they located him. So black fathers became invisible men, disappearing even from the census. They dropped out of the population while fairly young and didn't reappear until much later.

For years the welfare rolls reflected the employment situation almost directly. When there was a shortage of jobs, welfare went up; when jobs were plentiful, welfare went down. But toward the middle of the 1960s, this neat correlation fell apart. Fathers were leaving home whether they could find work or not. Some few may not have really disappeared at all, but parlayed welfare and low wages into a nearly decent living for their families. Others may have availed themselves of cheap divorces. How many middle-class fathers, upstanding types who put down welfare mothers, would leave their wives and kids without a qualm if they knew it wouldn't cost them a nickel? For whatever reasons, ghetto families took a beating — not only black families, but Puerto Ricans and Chicanos as well.

Ghetto youngsters became a vulnerable population, an afflicted population, likely to act out in any number of self-destructive ways. What many chose, in communities with a long history of druggism, was drugs.

Drug use starts early in the ghetto. Marijuana is common in junior high school, even in grade school. A teacher who asked three eleven-year-olds why they had gotten high was told simply that a marijuana cigarette costs fifty cents, "and what else can the three of us do for fifty cents?" There isn't the elaborate pharmacology of the suburbs. Marijuana and heroin are the only widely used drugs, with cocaine a luxury item for older, more sophisticated types. Starting out "snorting" (inhaling the heroin), youngsters can carry on undetected for quite a while. "It's easier to snort a bag of dope than it is to smoke a joint," one young user explained. "You can actually sit in the back of the classroom and hold the bag open and put your head under the desk and snort." Even when they are "chipping" (shooting heroin only on weekends), many youngsters can keep up with the minimal demands of most ghetto schools. Only when they are shooting several times a day does their drug use become apparent. In New York City, with its large population of heroin users, young addicts are rarely suspended from school. They can be arrested if they are actually caught with either the drugs or their works (the needle, eyedropper, and other paraphernalia), but usually the most that happens is that their parents are informed of the school's suspicions. So they stay in school until their drug needs become heavy enough to demand full-time criminal activity, and then they drop out or deal drugs in the school until they are caught.

Druggism is no longer unique to the poor, the socially handicapped, and the ghetto-raised. There are other vulnerable populations. White youngsters, middle-class youngsters, kids from families that are fairly solid and together are also using drugs. What these groups have in common is social superfluity. There is scarcely more room in our economy for white young people than there is for many blacks, Puerto Ricans, and Chicanos.

We don't put our middle-class children out on the street. We send them to school — endlessly. The average youngster who would have gotten just past eighth grade thirty years ago now finishes high school. Seven million are in college, and that total should hit ten million by 1980. Schooling is youth's busy-work, what we push at them when they complain, "We've got nothing to do."

To make this absurd system work, we have created educational requirements that have little to do with any real job demands. We have reinvented the Mandarin system, by which Chinese emperors chose administrators for their knowledge of classical literature. Industry plays happily along with this nonsense, using the universities to screen their employees. When a state university offers a master's degree in greenhouse management, the people who own glass houses will soon begin to demand master's degrees of their employees. The result is that more and more young people stay in school longer and longer, earning more degrees and higher degrees, which then become the requirements for jobs they could probably have filled before they entered college. Meanwhile — and this is where it hurts — the kids are kept dependent and, in a real sense, prevented from growing up.

Adolescence is a vulnerable time, humanity's chronological weak point, when youngsters are busily metamorphosing into adults. Instead of whisking our children past this trouble spot, we hold them there interminably. By keeping them dependent, denying them real jobs and real purpose or any way to make it on their own, we turn youth into a trap, a holding pattern for life within which nothing *real* happens. There are no real challenges, no real rewards.

There never used to be a stage of life called "youth." There were children and grown-ups, and in between something brief and awkward known as adolescence, which nobody paid much attention to until early in this century. It was once a fairly neat and simple arrangement. Boys and girls were equipped for sex just before they got their full growth. By then, they were ready, able, and allowed to take on an adult share of the workload and claim an adult's reward.

Sexual maturity now arrives way ahead of schedule. A seventeenth-century writer noted that menstruation rarely occurred before seventeen or eighteen in rural Austria, and in 1840, girls in Manchester, England, were ready just before they turned sixteen. Since then, however, the age of menarche, when girls first menstruate, has dropped two to five years and is now between twelve and thirteen for girls in the United States and Western Europe. (Although it was once thought that lasses ripen more rapidly under a hot sun, the facts disprove this theory. Nigerian girls first menstruate when they are past fourteen, only about two months earlier than the average Eskimo girl. Early sexual maturity seems to be more closely related to better nutrition.) Adolescence in America, then, gets stretched at both ends. There are girls in grade school today who are perfectly capable of becoming mothers and may go on to be graduate students at twenty-two or twenty-three, still tied to their parents.

With adolescence stretching on endlessly before them, maturity eluding them year after year, young people will often lash out with understandable rage at their chronic frustration. "Grow up," we tell them, when we really only want them to be better-behaved children. We are stunned when they choose to drop out, opt out, or cop out, as though a state of enforced youth is somehow normal and they are behaving abnormally.

To keep our youngsters in line, we bribe them. The economy too overdeveloped to use them has made most of us rich enough to buy time with our kids by loading them down with things. Part of the economy, in fact, depends upon a "youth market." But there are limits to bribery, and many parents today have few other resources. They are not well equipped to handle the hostile prisoners of protracted adolescence. The family itself is not the muscular social unit it once was. Back when everything was simpler, the family included a supporting network of relatives (the extended family). There was always a spare grandparent to watch the infants or an uncle to go a few rounds with the adolescents. To become more socially and geographically mobile, the family stripped down to a nuclear model — Mother, Father, and the kids. It is a more convenient travel unit, but not one that provides much strength. These mobile families usually live in large metropolitan areas, where the common concern of small communities for their young is missing. The irony is that parents are today up against the hardest job any generation ever faced, and they must handle it with less support than any of their predecessors had.

There is some idea that young people can be driven to drugs by what amounts to a sense of political despair, that the war in Vietnam, the existence of poverty and racism, immoralities and inequalities, have pushed many youngsters over the line. There may be some logic to this, but it has considerably less to do with the alienation of the kids than the confusion and ambivalence of their parents.

A good number of parents are confused about where they stand today. They believe in law and order and are repulsed by police violence. They are dismayed when their government resists changes. Their faith in America as the champion of the downtrodden has been shaken by our role as the protector of privilege and corruption in Vietnam. They have faithfully tried to follow conventional wisdom about child-rearing and become confused as it swings back and forth between the doctrines of strict control and ultimate permissiveness.

Youngsters are not naturally moral. They have gone along with societies that were markedly more repugnant than ours, accepted imperfections far more gross. Hitler's youth was all for the Führer and the Fatherland. But they were well conditioned. The message they got from their families, their schools, and the state-run media was clear and unanimous, and they bought it. What a great many parents today cannot do is make sense for their children out of what does not make sense for them. They cannot create order for their youngsters from the chaos of conflicting information. They transmit their own confusion, their own uncertainties. When their kids act out, their behavior is caused in part by their anger or resentment at their parents for failing to provide that guidance.

Parents can transmit helpful messages, without denying or concealing their own feelings. They can and should express distress with inequality, with the things they believe are inconsistent with their notions of what our nation should be. They can share their feelings in terms of what must be done and what can be done. Then they demonstrate concern, not confusion; action, not despair.

When families are holding together, or even one parent has himself or herself in hand, they can put up a good fight for their youngsters' heads. Parents who hope to overcome the social dislocation of the ghetto, the frustration of prolonged adolescence, and the muddles of our time must stay in close touch with their children. They must start early to form sound, consistent attitudes, preparing youngsters to face up to all they are going to run into and most of what will run into them — and drugs are only a part of it.

4. Starting Out Straight

THERE HAS ALWAYS BEEN a certain fascination with the idea of the "bad seed," the child who just can't grow straight. But few psychiatrists today seriously believe in the existence of the "psychopathic inferior." Yet we know that some children are born with physical differences that make their development difficult at best. Hyperactive children, for example, are rougher to handle from the beginning. They are screaming and thrashing about in the hospital nursery, while others are lying there calm and placid. But the factors that truly determine what becomes of these children, or all children, are factors that fortunately most parents can control.

Most adults have no memory at all of what life was like before they turned seven. This is a normal kind of amnesia, and they are unlikely to recall that early time unless they are psychoanalyzed. But those years before seven are terribly critical. Those are the years when children develop most of the attitudes they use for the rest of their lives, when they learn how to deal with other people.

Children are constantly tossing out clues to their developing attitudes. The mother of a three-year-old girl recently brought her new baby son home from the hospital. The daughter watched as mother diapered the infant. There was a knife nearby, and the little girl picked it up. "Put down the knife," her mother ordered. The child hesitated. "Mommy," she said, "let's peel him."

There are parents who would ignore an incident like this, or convince themselves that the little girl was making a joke. After all, she wouldn't actually *hurt* the baby. Such parents are just not registering the noises they hear for the signals they are. If they were driving down the road and began hearing funny sounds from under the hood, they'd stop their car fast enough and find out what was wrong. Young children also send out explicit distress signals, but the average father is more sensitive to the needs of his car and the average mother to her washing machine.

What's going on inside that little head is a painful accommodation to the existence of other people and other people's needs. For his first year and a half, a child sees his mother merely as an extension of himself. Only at eighteen months does he get the idea that his body ends at one point and his mother's starts somewhere else. Yet, because of his helplessness, he continues to see those around him in terms of his own needs.

During the attitude-forming years, the child's major conflict is with the world beyond himself that doesn't respond quickly enough to what "me" wants and what "me" wants *now*. One of the first tasks of parents, then, is helping "me" to cope with a world that doesn't allow for instant gratification most of the time.

Unless parents have a fairly good idea of what's going on inside their youngster's head and a realistic view of their own behavior, they can make a sorry botch of this assignment. Suppose Mother is teaching her daughter not to grab food off the table, but to wait until her dinner has been served. The child is hungry and she wants to grab. So, Mother lays down a rule: "Don't grab." The rule is good, but the real key to the lesson is the way Mother herself behaves. When parents lay down a rule, they can punish the child each time it is broken. But more important is the reinforcement that comes when parents follow their rules themselves. The reverse is also true. The whole "don't grab" lesson falls apart when the little girl watches

Mother snatching dresses off the rack during a department store sale or shoving into line because she's double-parked outside the market.

The parents whose little girl wanted to peel her baby brother had run up against a common childhood crisis. Most children have siblings, brothers or sisters or both. And each new arrival is legitimate cause for anxiety. Even siblings who never arrive are a threat; many only children live in constant fear that something or somebody is going to come and take some of what they have away.

When a new baby is on the scene, the two- or three-year-old's worst fears are realized. Mother is giving attention and love and care to the new one. It is a painful thing for the older child to watch, and one of his first reactions is an urge to annihilate that baby. There is nothing abnormal about this feeling. It would be strange for a three-year-old to react any other way.

Now, Mother and Father have a rough job to do. They have to get through to that older child and make him understand that he can't kill the baby, that he must be loving and gentle with the younger, more helpless one. If they try to pressure the child, make him swallow a lot of nonsense about how "we all love the baby" and how "we only cuddle the little sweetie pie," they deny completely the conflict inside the child. He still has no way of knowing what to do about all those feelings that urge him to hurt the little interloper.

The alternative is for the parents to play it straight with the older child, tell him that they understand it's difficult for him, they know how much *he* wants to be the baby. That way, the three-year-old has no undigested knot of feelings left down deep inside. He has gotten his feelings out and his parents have helped him to deal with them. Now, the parents can make a reasonable demand that, in spite of his feelings, he *act* in gentle ways toward his new brother or sister. At the same time, parents have to be aware that part of the rejection the older child is feeling may be very real. If they have been less than gentle with him, it's a bit much to ask him to be gentle with the new arrival.

We keep coming back to the hoary adage that the apple doesn't fall very far from the tree, and kids, by and large, develop at least the initial set of attitudes that their parents display. You can't hand your offspring a set of standards you aren't able to live with yourself and not create some serious confusion in his head. What does a youngster make of it when he's riding with his parents, and Mother is complaining about how fast Father is driving? Then there are sirens and a traffic cop leaning into the car and Father is lying his head off. "Why, Officer, I wasn't speeding. The needle was right there on fifty."

Kids pick up all kinds of dishonesty. But it is most painful when they catch their parents up in emotional dishonesty, directed toward them. The child can recognize the signs of various feelings in his parents. He senses when something is making his father or mother angry. So he asks, "Are you angry?" And a sound comes back: "Oh, no, what would make you think that I was angry?" But the child really knows what his parents feel by the way they act. When his father says, "Of course I love you, Johnny," Johnny knows that Daddy is talking through his hat. He doesn't spend time with Johnny, doesn't include his son in what he's doing, isn't sensitive to how Johnny feels at any particular time. In many ways, he demonstrates to Johnny that he is not concerned. There is a big gap between what Father is saying and what he is telling his son in far more effective ways.

Parents don't confuse their children intentionally. They may not even understand why they are doing the very things that are making problems for their youngsters. Most people cannot really explain much about their behavior, why they do what they do. They can give you reasons, because they believe they really know. That's what makes it so hard to get people in touch with the real motivations for their behavior.

In a mother-daughter relationship where the mother (because of a psychological template impressed by *her* mother) is troubled by her sexuality, she will pass this on to her child. The little girl is just beginning to experiment with lipstick, high heels, and such things, and Mother tells her this is wrong. The child wants to know why. "Why, Mommy, why can't I do that? Other ladies look pretty."

What Mother does then is to hand her child some bit of pseudologic. She may say, "That's not nice. Little girls don't do that." But other little girls are doing it, and the child sees other women dressing up and being pleasing to men. It now becomes very difficult for that little girl to understand part of her feminine role.

To make it more confusing, Mother isn't always consistent about the way she behaves. She may use her sexuality or her femininity, to manipulate Father. The child is then in a real bind. Her mother has a problem and the little girl inherits it. Because of Mother's inconsistency, she can't even learn how to handle that problem. It's like trying to understand the rules of a game when the rules are constantly changing.

Parents needn't understand all their motives; they don't have to know why they behave the way they do in every case. Their behavior may not always be logical, but if it makes no trouble for them or for their children, there is probably no need to analyze it. Indeed, most parents cannot spot their own inconsistencies. If, however, they do seem to be raising a confused or unhappy child, the parents will have to consider the influence of their actions. They can find out what is bothering the youngster and backtrack from there.

All of this makes being a parent sound like a gigantic egg walk. It needn't be. In fact, there are dangers to overcaution. The goal is not some kind of programmed, dehumanized parents who have no feelings — or at least never show them to their children. Parents can sometimes become so self-conscious with their young that they choke up, with the result that the children choke up, too. Everyone is tripping over everyone else trying to do the right thing, and that's really useless.

We are not dealing with orchids, but with little human beings who are amazingly tough. Life is a series of problems and contradictions, disappointments and distress, and the human spirit is marvelously resilient. Given a certain amount of support and encouragement, your child can survive just about anything.

Parents are going to make mistakes. They are going to feed confusing and contradictory information to their children. Yet the children will survive all of this, if the parents tune in early enough to what their youngsters are thinking and feeling.

Parents should be understanding. But this does not in any way imply that they shouldn't be realistic and demanding. Some parents equate understanding with tolerating all kinds of behavior, not making any demands. If the child is angry and he wants to break things up, let him break them up. He is a little bit unhappy about his new sibling, so let him draw with crayons all over the walls and work it out. He is sad when Mommy goes away on a vacation without him, and when she comes back she finds that two of her favorite dresses have been cut up with little scissors. Parents who make allowances for this kind of behavior are preventing their children from learning how to cope with frustration or stress in rational ways.

There is a difference between understanding the way a child feels and making clear the ways in which he's expected to behave. These have to be specific. It's not fair to demand a level of performance that hasn't been carefully spelled out — and enforced. Enforcement, however, cannot be a license for cruelty. Punishment must be administered in tolerable doses, firmly but not harshly, with a knowledge of how much the child can handle. Making a three-year-old girl stand in the corner for an hour is plainly cruel. But telling her to get up and leave the table for three minutes may make a great deal of sense.

Children really want to learn all the rules. It's not hard to make them into the kind of youngsters you want to have around the house, for that's what they are working to become. From about six through twelve, they are busy becoming little socialized adults.

What sort of little adults (and eventually big adults) they become depends upon the kinds of information they are fed. Not all of that information comes from their parents, but when children are fairly young, Mother and Father have a big advantage. If they use it well, they can keep channels open later on, when the outside competition gets much heavier. Once again, the quick, easy way is disastrous. Parents cannot expect to be able to influence their children at critical points in their lives if they haven't put in time with them at every point along the way. There aren't any short cuts to being a good parent.

It is especially difficult for fathers to find the time to make that vital input. When they don't, they often compound the problem; they look for an easy way to get rid of the guilt feelings they have about shortchanging their youngsters. The classic mistake is to try and buy their way out. They come home disturbed, feeling they have been withholding something from their children, and then attempt to purchase a peaceful conscience by bringing home a big present. Or they give the children special privileges. They say, "Tonight, Johnny can stay up an extra hour." They let Jane cop out on her homework. In order to restore their own good feelings, they will break down discipline, undermine all that their wives have been trying to do.

An insecure father, worried about making up for lost time, tends to overdo it. Being a good parent doesn't mean you have to be a child. You don't have to get down and play dolls with your daughter or get into your son's little wagon. Kids don't want this. If you try to tell them, "I'm your friend," they will set you straight right off: "You're not my friend; you're my daddy." They don't want that kind of familiarity. What they do want is some distance. They want you to set the rules. And they want you to be there, to be available, and to include them in some of the things you do. There's a necessary balance between how much they do with you and how much they do by themselves.

There are fathers who come home overworked and anxious, fathers who have few friends of their own and try to make buddies out of their children. They don't want distance between themselves and their children. They won't put any demands on their children that will create distance. These fathers aren't concerned with the needs of their children. They are using the children to meet their own needs.

The ways in which parents handle their own needs, how they deal with stress, what they do when they are sad or angry — these are major chunks of data that children take in and register. When Mother is angry with Father, how does she deal with her anger? Does she avoid it? Does she drink, or pop pills, or eat too much? If she does, she is giving her offspring a violent shove toward druggism.

You can lose your temper, you can get angry. There are times when Mother and Father can yell at each other. It is not always unhealthy for children to see their parents argue, but it is important that parents fight fair — that nobody gets hurt, nobody goes away. In other words, there has to be agreement that when a conflict arises, both parents can talk, both can yell, and, even if no resolution is reached, nobody walks out. Children shouldn't see one-sided attacks or arguments that are out of control. They shouldn't be exposed to violence, threats of violence, or threats of abandonment.

Abandonment is a real fear, a continuing threat to most children. In many ways, it is as great a fear as that of a parent's dying; for death, to a child, is the ultimate abandonment. When he sees a dead squirrel or bird, or learns that a friend's father has died, he says to himself: "If that can happen to the bird or the squirrel or my friend's father, it can happen to me or to my father or my mother." And then, "Who will take care of me?" When he fears that one of his parents may leave home, a child suffers the same anxieties, wondering what will become of him, who will take care of him.

Sometimes a child's fears of abandonment become reality — his parents get divorced. This experience needn't be an unqualified disaster for the child. In many cases it is his salvation, for it is doubtful that a youngster has much to gain or learn in a home where conflicts are serious enough to result in divorce. He can come through the experience strengthened if, again, his parents are sensitive to his feelings — and if they do not try to use him or manipulate him into acting out their own wishes for revenge.

The divorced parent cannot burden the child with his own needs. He must understand that more important than a child's loyalties is his absolute dependence, his concern about "who's going to take care of me." The helplessness a child feels totally victimizes him. If he remains with his mother and she chooses to put Daddy down, the child is going to have to buy this. He's not going to be able to hold in his heart the truth that Daddy is really a fine fellow. He has to go with the party line, to believe it, because that's what Mother says. He is now dependent entirely upon his mother, and he can't afford to cross her. This is the most damaging result of a divorce. It is particularly harmful when the mother is disturbed or even psychotic, because the child must buy a psychotic party line. What happens to a boy of eight or ten when his mother makes this kind of demand on him?

The boy loved his father, who was warm and sensitive and great to be with. All of a sudden, he must swallow the idea that Daddy was cold and selfish. He already has some angry feelings because his father has left him, and these feelings are perfectly normal. Instead of helping him to work out these feelings, so that he can understand the anger he has for his father, Mother uses them. She denies the reality and inflicts her own distorted mental set on the child. This kind of behavior does more than destroy the boy's relationship with his father. It affects his relationships with everybody. He becomes incapable of perceiving how people really are because his machinery for that kind of perception has been so badly damaged.

If the child of such a divorce is a girl and she receives the same distorted imprint, it can be even more harmful. If the false Daddy she is forced to accept becomes the prototype for all men, she will have great difficulties with her femininity, for every man she meets will be seen as an enemy.

There are influences other than parents that work on a child's attitudes as he marches through latency toward adolescence. If parents, schools, and friends all share common values, as they do in the Soviet Union, then all these forces reinforce and buttress each other. But in our society, parents can be made completely ineffectual by these forces; the deck is stacked against them. Yet they do have one good card to play if they have kept the channels open and are listening for what their youngsters are feeling — which is not always the same as what they are saying.

When the youngster goes off to school, he comes into contact with teachers, most of whom are fairly young. Not all of these teachers have settled into their adult identities, and their attitudes tend to be different from those at home. They may present views on sex or drugs or ways of living that are quite opposed to the views of the family.

The child finds even more different views when he gets into books. And as he makes friends, he finds these peers will debunk both his parents' views and his teachers' views. If the child is receiving a religious education, this is added to the mix, and were he to turn to the media — to newspapers, magazines, and television — the multiplicity of attitudes would increase tenfold.

Before you get the idea that your child is being hopelessly buffeted about by tidal waves of information, remember that he has been handling a fairly massive input since infancy. He will survive it, just as you do, by tuning most of it out. What's important for you to keep in mind is that he does have sources of information other than his parents. You can't limit what he learns. And you can't legitimately ask, "Now where did Johnny pick that up?" But you can guide him, you can help him absorb it, and you can make sure you don't add to his problems by feeding him more indigestible data.

Fathers often make this mistake — giving a youngster more information than he asks for. When a three-year-old child asks, "Where do babies come from?" he isn't after a graphic description of sexual relations. The answer is: "From Mommy's stomach." The child who can depend on his father to give him information he can understand will keep turning to his father when things confuse him. But if Daddy bombards him with complex material he can't understand, he'll learn to tune Daddy out. If you can be sensitive enough to answer the questions your child asks at the level he asks them, then you can help him to grow, rather than inhibiting his growth with overstimulation.

Eventually you will have to help your child make painful discoveries. Having access to so many sources of information, he'll get the message quite early that the world is not all of a piece, that there is injustice and inconsistency throughout.

If you've laid the groundwork, he can handle it. Part of that preparation is dealing honestly with situations at home. When he complains that his younger brother is bothering him, listen to him. It is true that younger brothers or sisters invade and complicate the lives of older children and their relationships with their parents. But an older child can come to accept the injustice if he is shown that the younger child has needs that are just as strong as his own.

The task of communicating with children is, even for the most sensitive and intelligent families, a staggering one. It has never been more difficult, because today's parents are pitted against the whole technology of communications. When you think you have done a fairly decent job of answering your children's questions, sensing their feelings, and meeting their needs, they slip over the border of childhood into adolescence. And it's Round Two.

5. The Adolescent Storm

IN SPITE OF ALL THE WEIGHT we put on the parents' role, we know most kids can do a pretty decent job of growing up without much help. Unless some kind of sick imprint is etched upon their minds, by their families or by the world, they stand a good chance of making it through intact. But as youngsters come roaring into adolescence, it suddenly seems that everything they've gotten together is falling apart.

That little socialized human being who has been hanging around the house for twelve or more years and learned manners, speech, and a set of imitative attitudes, suddenly becomes a confused young person. All at once, the barriers start to break down and he loses control. His body is going through some profound changes, and so are his feelings.

Those changes start in the glands and in the genitals. But adolescence is more than just the onset of sexuality. During adolescence, one reaches physical maturity in all ways, growing out of the body of a child and into that of an adult. While these things are happening to him, the adolescent is learning how to cope with his new maturity, finding ways to assert himself. Ideally, the struggle results in a real firming up of the youngster's identity, so that he ends adolescence knowing who he is.

It's not easy to find out who you are. You have to fight for that kind of knowledge, because you start into adolescence without much of an identity. A relatively healthy kid has gone along and bought the family's party line. It may not always seem that way, because smart youngsters play all kinds of intellectual games and try to catch their parents on inconsistencies. But there is no real critical thought at work here. The younger child is too aware of his helplessness for that. He isn't about to challenge seriously the people he knows he needs to take care of him. With adolescence, though, the youngster begins to lose this fear. By the time he is full-grown and physically able to care for himself, he has developed the resolve to break through the party line, to declare his individuality. This causes a lot of turmoil and confusion. But if the resolve is strong enough and if the youngster is healthy enough, it will lead to an acceptance of adulthood, the successful completion of adolescence. When the struggle is hidden, when "Johnny never gives us a bit of trouble," because he has bottled up all his rebellion, then Johnny is headed for trouble. Somehow these feelings are going to have to come out, and they can come out in some sick ways. Johnny is like the good soldier, the professional private who is a weekend drunk because he can't handle his rage at himself and the people upon whom he is dependent.

Puberty begins earlier than it once did; the glands usually begin pumping away at the age of twelve. And most children are fully grown, physically mature, and physically capable of independence at fifteen. But they aren't completely aware of it yet, because one's mental view of himself always lags somewhere behind the physical reality. A new physical capacity, like a new technology, is effectively mastered only over a number of years.

Because of the social realities that force us to discount the capabilities of young people, adolescence doesn't usually come to term normally. Our society lacks the capacity to absorb its young in any functional way, and thus we inflict on them a prolonged period of dependency.

As long as young people remain dependent — both emotionally and financially — they can't really become psychologically mature, they can't finish growing up. They are always

The Adolescent Storm   47

measuring themselves against someone else's standards. An adult must stand on his own, with a function, a job, and a means of paying his way. Freud's definition of psychological health as "the ability to work and love productively" still stands up. A young person is ready to assume this maturity at seventeen or eighteen, but is generally prevented from doing so.

The eighteen-year-old is old enough to marry, have children, and be responsible. But in most cases, our society doesn't allow this, certainly not for middle-class youngsters, who have much longer to wait before they're cut loose. They remain dependent and their adolescence is extended well into their twenties — or later. Someone who is aiming at a career in medicine can remain dependent into his thirties.

One of the ironies of this situation is that our older students, who are still functioning dependently, are not functioning nearly as well as they might. They are too involved in getting things right, in pleasing someone else. Even when they do get it right, when they pass their tests and make good grades, they still miss a lot of material they would have picked up if they weren't dominated by a raging concern to win the approval of the parents or teachers upon whom they depend. They are constantly demanding: "Tell me I'm doing okay. Mark me."

It may not always seem that way, but the large adolescent throwing his new-grown weight around the house is looking for approval. Both rebellion and dependency with its need for approval can coexist in the same youngster. This isn't new; the rebellion has been there since early childhood. Small children often try to do things their own way, but are usually too frightened, too helpless to be very insistent in their attempts at independence. Fighting the family establishment, the parents, starts early, but it's not very successful or very intense until adolescence.

The parallel need for rebellion and approval produces some ludicrous situations. One boy who dropped out of school when he was fifteen moved out of the house but continued to bring his problems home to his parents. He was a bright lad, and big, and had more than enough musical talent to become independent if he finished his schooling. His parents didn't believe he was doing himself any good, and could hardly approve of his actions, but the boy wanted their approval and kept coming home to get it. What he was really saying was: "I want you to continue to support me, but I don't want to live by your rules and regulations, whether it's wearing clean clothes or cutting my hair or going to school or living at home. I don't want to do any of these things, but I want you to take care of me and to approve of me."

Most adolescents don't move out; they stay and fight it out on the family's home ground. They will come in bombastically and announce, "I'm independent. I don't have to think your way." They'll challenge their parents on ideological grounds: "You say you are really interested in the poor, but look at you sitting there eating a steak instead of beans." They will hack away at restrictions: "I'm old enough to decide how I dress, or when I come home, or if I have to study." And between these bursts of assertion there are little whimpering noises that say, "Take care of me. I'm afraid. What am I going to do?" It's easier for girls to express these feelings of need. It's permissible for girls to come home to Mother periodically, even after they're grown, to be petted and encouraged. For a young man, it's harder to get these messages across. The need for reassurance is not considered manly, and some fathers who want to deny their own fearfulness, or forget their days of dependency, won't accept that kind of behavior from their sons.

When all this action is going on, when your adolescent is raging around, you have to recognize how important it is for him to explore independence. He does it badly, awkwardly, because he hasn't had any practice. That's what he's doing with you — practicing. The reason he keeps challenging your ideas is because they are *your* ideas, and he's trying to work out his own. So when he comes on ready to fight, give him room to develop his ideas, to follow through. Then, don't hit him the next time he's vulnerable, when he needs support or is a little bit fearful.

Unfortunately, when some youngsters challenge hard, they provoke parents who may be particularly tough or rigid, who are not really listening to *all* the messages coming from their youngsters. Once provoked, these parents will really bang away at the child with a lot more power than is necessary, forcing the adolescent to give up trying to talk the problem through and get some resonance from them.

The parent who takes the adolescent's challenge too literally, who has to make it clear from the start that he is right, invites more worrisome troubles. The youngster wants to take on the old man about drugs, and the old man cuts him off and starts laying down the law: "You bring any of that stuff in my house, I'm going to break your goddamn head," or, "That's all you and your damn friends are interested in," or, "Why don't you grow up?" Well, that's just what the boy is trying to do if the old man would just shut up and give him a chance. Parents who take this pugnacious stance may force their kids to go a step further than talking, which is to act out some of these ideas.

Being a parent to the adolescent is really not much different from raising his younger brothers and sisters. You have got to listen to what he says and what he means and what he feels. Listening and understanding do not necessarily mean that you have to agree or approve. But the act of listening is a kind of demonstration of faith. When a parent lets his adolescent express his thoughts and opinions about drugs, he is saying that he believes in the youngster and knows that he is sensible enough not to become involved in drug use.

If Father gets hit with an ideological challenge, he does not really need to make any big speeches — the kid knows where he stands. If Father has done his job for the past ten years, his child is aware of what he feels about drugs, alcohol, religion and race, peace and the poor. He has demonstrated a humanistic value system that makes sense.

But what about a real threat? What happens when a youngster decides to quit school? If you go deeply into what he feels, you can probably find plenty to understand. You may even agree that much of what he is studying is worthless and the teachers are wasting his time. But you needn't accept his plan to drop out, although there are times when parents may decide a young boy or girl could profit from a semester at something other than school. Just by listening to his beefs, understanding, giving him a chance to vent some of his feelings, you have reduced the pressure on the youngster, diminished his need to act. This is a psychological constant. If someone is angry at you and you can get him to tell you, "I feel like punching you in the face," you have considerably reduced the chances of being punched in the face.

At bottom line, if talking and understanding have failed to resolve an issue, then parents may have to use their muscle. Their youngster still wants to live at home and continue to enjoy the warmth and security there. This gives parents a mighty edge in enforcing compliance.

More than the younger child, the adolescent leans on his peer group, the other youngsters he runs with, his friends. Adolescents can't tell everything to their parents. They need secrets, they need distance, and they need a wider audience to try their ideas and attitudes on. In some ways, the peer group is in competition with the family, but the adolescent needs both. If your child doesn't seem to have one, to belong to one, you'd better try and figure out why.

There are some things youngsters cannot and should not discuss with their parents. These are intimate concerns, like pimples and poetry, erections and love. He cannot discuss these things with his family. He might talk with an older brother about them, although even that is difficult if he feels the information will get back to his parents. He is usually most comfortable discussing these things with his friends.

The adolescent needs to use his peer group because it has a particular sensitivity to him. The other youngsters share his awkwardness, his sense of frustration, his fears — the whole range of very intense feelings that adolescents go through. Parents are really quite removed from all of this because most of them have forgotten how really ghastly it was to be stood up on a date or to break up with a steady. Peers do understand and can help.

There are dangers in the peer-group situation. Adolescents are very vulnerable to camaraderie, and the values of the group tend to be infectious. If the group's way of dealing with anger at their parents is to steal cars or use drugs, it is difficult for an individual youngster to resist going along.

If the peer group is destructive, parents must move fast — and ruthlessly, if necessary. If they've kept the channels open, are really in touch with their child, they stand a good chance of severing a destructive relationship without bringing all their muscle into play. Sure, he'll kick and scream, "They're my friends," and if he is unwilling to find new ones, then his parents will have to move him off the scene, to a new school or out of town for a long stay with friends or relatives. This is a real crisis and should be handled as one.

There's a chance that it isn't Junior's peers who are making him act in various antisocial ways, but Junior himself. If this is the case, shipping Junior out of town doesn't help at all. Druggism usually starts with a group experience, but that doesn't mean that the group induces anyone to become a drug user. No youngster who isn't already seriously troubled is going to be a passive prisoner of the group. Still, almost every drug-troubled youngster is shipped off, at one time or another, for the "geographic cure." The idea is to get him away from dangerous peers, but the trouble is that in many cases Junior is his own worst friend.

Not all acting out is dangerous or illegal. Suppose a youngster is under intense pressure. His teachers are coming down hard on him at school, his old man is coming down hard at home. He is angry most of the time and may get some relief by knocking himself out on the basketball court or running around the track. These are ways of acting out his problems, but they offer only temporary relief. The youngster really needs to confront the problems, handle them verbally, get some understanding, and resolve them. Then he might be able to enjoy basketball or track without being driven to it. Once he gets his head straight, he will probably be a better athlete. Until then, he stands a good chance of twisting his ankle or stumbling over the hurdle in his anger at his father or his teachers.

Often, when adolescents have trouble handling their sexuality or their aggression, they pick far more destructive ways to act than throwing themselves into basketball. They steal, drink, take obvious physical risks. They go to these dangerous lengths because the need for adventure and the need to be a hero are also important parts of adolescence.

A confused adolescent may turn to drugs because they seem to fulfill his need for adventure. An LSD trip is a voyage into new and mysterious areas. The activity surrounding drug use is a cops-and-robbers game, which involves the intrigue of making the purchase and the very intimate ritual of drug taking.

The dangers of adolescence seem overwhelming, but to the extent that family relationships have been strong and healthy, the youngster will survive the turbulence, the challenges, and the anger. Where there have been no such bonds, but instead a sense of frustration and abandonment, he has no mooring in all this turbulence, nothing to hang on to.

6. Dealing with Drugs

SHOWING LOVE, concern, and responsibility to adolescents means meeting their challenges openly, comforting them when they falter, and reassuring them when they are afraid. Adolescence is a season of difficult changes, and family influence drops to zero if parents try to stifle the discord or squelch independent outbursts. Youngsters under this kind of gag rule lose touch with home base and turn to their peers for support. By encouraging your children to sound off, you can handle parent-child conflict so that it leads to real growth.

Drugs are a natural, an almost certain source of controversy. If the issue is never raised, then either yours is a rare and fortunate community or, more likely, the atmosphere in your home is not open and free enough for your children to talk about what they are really feeling. Most youngsters have strong feelings about drugs, uncertainties if not opinions. Even adolescents who do not use drugs, who have no intention of ever using drugs, will take up the battle for the right of their drug-using peers to do their thing.

If you have encouraged realistic attitudes all along and lived by them yourself, your children already have a good idea of where you stand on drugs. It isn't necessary, or even useful, to spell out every detail of what you believe before drugs become a reality in their lives. You can't just grab hold of your youngsters some rainy Saturday afternoon, because you feel the dope menace may be lurking about, and launch into a long lecture. You should feed them information bit by bit, as they ask for it.

Children catch on quickly. They don't need many clues. They learn a lot from the way you dole out medicine when they are infants. Some mothers will dose Baby with aspirin when Baby has a runny nose and a temperature of 99.5 degrees, because Baby is cranky, and when Baby gets cranky Mother becomes irritated. So Mother seeks relief by giving *Baby* medicine. This is exactly what many doctors do when they prescribe drugs that may not be specifically indicated for any physical complaint but will produce a desired psychological or social effect. Mother gives Baby aspirin, Baby quiets down, and Mother feels less irritated.

Parents often feel they must *do something* about their children's every discomfort. Unless they are dispensing cough syrup, nose drops, or teething gel, they believe they are being remiss. Somehow, just spending time with the child, comforting him, doesn't seem enough. What if Grandmother should call and learn her grandchild is feeling poorly? "What are you doing?" she demands. "What are you *giving* him?" Children from such families grow to expect a pharmacological response to their every ache and pain. Because Mother may feel guilty or unloving if she isn't giving something for her child's distress, the child comes to demand these little tokens of her love.

The harried mother, busy or distracted, may go one step further and provide medication *in place of* the attention she is unable to supply just then. Understandably, this habit increases her offspring's appetite for these symbols of Mother's concern — the candy-coated medicaments, children's aspirin, children's vitamins, and cough syrups. Flavored medication for the young has made this much simpler. It is easy to substitute candy for kisses, but pushing castor oil for love is somewhat more difficult, and children would probably be less likely to accept a chemical replacement for affection if that replacement were particularly horrid-tasting.

Mothers who feel secure about the way they are doing their job and the amount of emotional sustenance they are providing their youngsters are less likely to hand out drugs casually. But the family's doctor may give Mother no choice. If her child is a clinic patient, in and out in three minutes, there is a greater chance of Mother's being handed a prescription than if her child is treated by a private pediatrician who can spend a reasonable amount of time with mother and child. Since he can clearly demonstrate his concern this way, he feels less need to medicate.

Parents sometimes end up treating imaginary illnesses with real remedies. Children can decide to play sick when they want to stay home from school and will complain of a sore throat or bellyache. Often Mother senses that there is something else going on, that her child isn't really sick, but she just may not be up to the struggle of packing him off to school. She compounds the situation by providing medication for his imagined ills. Now everybody is confused. The child feels guilty for what he has done, but Mother's medicine has legitimatized his ailment, and he is really worried, asking himself, "Doesn't she know that I'm not really sick?"

It is important, in a situation like this, to find out *why* the child wanted to stay home. Once again, we come up against the need to listen to what children are saying. What is he telling you when he plays sick on a school-day morning? You have to hear out the complaints and try to pin down the trouble. At first he may not tell you exactly what is bothering him, and if it is serious enough the situation will come up again. But you asked and you listened; that's what counts. When you then say, "Okay, now, you've got to finish dressing and hustle off to school," the child may make a face before leaving, but he will be much relieved that you have responded to the real problem — not the imaginary one.

Young children accept drugs as magic because everything is rather magical to them. If parents seem to regard drugs the same way, then the kids will build on this magical notion and develop their own fantasies about drugs, about the wonderful things that drugs can do for them and make them become. It is possible for a child to develop a strong predisposition toward druggism by the time he is six.

Your attitude about drugs becomes clear to your children quite early, by what you give or don't give them and by what you take yourself. To keep from confusing the child, both parents had better swing much the same way. You can't have Mother withholding aspirin and Father gobbling tranquilizers. This doesn't mean parents should parrot each other. In fact, if they have their act down too pat, their children won't buy it. Youngsters resist what sounds rehearsed and produced especially for their benefit.

Parents make mistakes and children still survive. If you have been openhanded with aspirin and cough syrup (and most young parents are), you haven't condemned your youngster to druggism. You can start late, when your child is eight or even older, to change the pattern. But your child must understand the change and see it as a consistent attitude about drugs. There is no point at which it is too late for parents to do *something*. But early attitudes carry a lot of weight and the later you wait to decide where you stand on drugs, the greater risk your youngster runs.

It is not possible to decide what you believe about drugs and make that attitude stick with your children unless you have already laid the groundwork with plenty of other attitudes. One way a child comes to understand what you feel about drugs (and, more important, *why* you feel that way) is through learning what you feel about other things. Parents provide that information by making specific judgments about all kinds of other behavior.

This is difficult for a great number of them. They fear sounding opinionated and unreasonable. At the back of their minds is the image of the Victorian father, that heavy-handed old

tyrant in chin whiskers. Making value judgments was easy ~
him; it was what he did best. Of course, nobody in the family
could challenge him. If the children demurred, no matter
how politely, they were ordered to their rooms or the woodshed,
depending upon the sex of the offender or the grievousness of
the offense.

Today we reject that autocratic old tartar and are generally
reluctant to make judgments that contradict other parents or
ideas our youngsters insist are common to the community. This
makes us suckers for the "everybody is doing it" blackmail, and
it doesn't much matter what it is "everybody" is doing: staying
up until midnight, watching television on school nights, biking
down the highway, going steady at twelve, cutting school on
Wednesday afternoons, or ultimately — smoking pot.

Parents today are often slow to condemn *their* peers, to say
flatly that other parents are plain wrong — that riding bicycles
on the highway is foolish and dangerous, that keeping kids up
past ten is ridiculous, and that what the Browns, Smiths, or
O'Briens choose to do is a matter of monumental unconcern.
Parents must sound off and say that they doubt other families
allow their youngsters to do such things — but if the Smiths
do, then the Smiths are wrong. By making judgments about
what other parents do, you prepare your children to make
judgments about what their peers are doing.

The difference between you and your Victorian forebear is
that the decisions you make are shared with your children. You
don't deliver ultimatums from a bank of darkened clouds, laying them down like divine law. Your judgments aren't arbitrary; you share the decision-making process with your kids,
giving them your reasoning about bedtimes, bicycles, and
television, and putting them into a better position to make
independent judgments of their own.

If you must err, then err on the side of rigidity. What children do *not* need is an open-minded relativist for a parent; his
ambivalence is far more terrifying than the rigid certainties of

an old-style, unbending moralist. The results of ambiguity are predictable. Students at a Connecticut high school were recently asked what their parents would do or say if they learned the youngsters were using drugs. The great majority replied that their parents would react strongly to such news. A smaller group believed their parents would not be very concerned. While less than one third of the entire student body had some drug-taking experience, about 95 percent of those in the smaller group said they had used drugs.

By the time your youngsters bring home their feelings, their uncertainties about drugs, you should be certain of your attitude and feel comfortable with it. No ambiguity is permitted. But discussion is encouraged, lots of discussion. There is real danger in cutting children off, and parents unprepared to deal with the subject often do just that. They shout NO to their children and then refuse to face the feedback. When parents cover their uncertainties this way, trying to avoid any discussion, they are arming the drug issue. By hearing the youngsters out, letting them explore their feelings and defend their ideas, they can defuse the issue. Here again, the need for action can be diminished by venting the situation, giving the steam, the pressure, a place to blow off. When this does not happen, when the drug conflict remains armed, it may blow up in tragic ways. For some young people, drugs become the focus of their struggle to be independent of their parents. Drug taking is seen as a rite of passage, a ceremony marking their freedom from childhood's chains.

A reasonable attitude about drugs must be one that parents believe, one they can hold and defend knowledgeably and one that they themselves can live with comfortably. But this attitude must be based on the understanding that *the habitual use of any psychoactive drug is destructive.*

It is only in instances of severe, chronic mental illness that the regular use of stimulants, depressants, antidepressants, tranquilizers, or sleeping pills is defensible. There is no reason for these medications to be in the family medicine chest. If Mother wants to lose weight, she can lose it without amphetamines. If Father has trouble sleeping, it is probably better to find out why he has this trouble than to dose him with sleeping pills.

Not *all* psychoactive substances must be barred from the home. If parents can live with a blanket prohibition, they should certainly do so. Most parents, however, use alcohol, a psychoactive drug that is often misused and responsible for the loss of more lives than all the other psychoactives combined. Yet alcohol, used moderately, can facilitate social interaction; it provides an experience that is pleasant and relaxing for most people.

The effect of marijuana is similar, and it is used by many adults in much the same way that alcohol is used. Like alcohol, it is also apt to be misused, and is as destructive when it is misused. While there is no absolute parallel — regular use of alcohol is more physically damaging, regular use of marijuana can be more psychologically disturbing — both of these psychoactives seem to be used safely by large numbers of adults. Note, we are dealing specifically with occasional use within a social setting for a social purpose — and that purpose is not to get looped, loaded, or stoned. It is certainly safer to steer clear of all psychoactives, and it is essential for some people. Former alcoholics know enough to stay away from liquor, and anyone with a history of drug misuse should be bright enough to leave marijuana alone. But if you choose to drink, you must accept the fact that, if it were legal, someone else might well choose to smoke pot. You needn't approve, but you can't very well condemn it, not without creating a damning inconsistency in your attitude about drugs. And that attitude must be reasonable and logical if you expect it to have any impact on your youngsters.

This does not mean that it is all right for adolescents to smoke marijuana, any more than it is all right for them to drink alcohol. There are different rules for adolescents because adolescents *are* different from adults. The nature of adolescence was well described by Anna Freud, who wrote: "I take it that it is normal for the adolescent to behave . . . in an inconsistent and unpredictable manner; to fight his impulses and to accept them; . . . to love his parents and to hate them; to revolt against them and to be dependent on them; . . . to thrive on imitation of and identification with others while searching unceasingly for his own identity; to be more idealistic, artistic, generous and unselfish than he will ever be again; but also the opposite, self-centered, egoistic and calculating."

Adolescents are suspended in the moment of change — insecure, uncertain, frightened, and more vulnerable than at any other time in their lives. If the process of change is disturbed, disrupted, then anxieties mount and the firming up of the identity, the purpose of all this turmoil, may never be completed, and no adult will emerge from the damaged chrysalis of adolescence.

The surge of hormones, the pressure of peers, the search for something to hang on to during their troubled passage — these make adolescents unlikely candidates for occasional social use of marijuana. Their needs are too great, their self-discipline to rudimentary — and it is too dangerous for them.

Drs. Harold Kolansky and William T. Moore found, as have other adolescent psychotherapists, that: "Marijuana accentuates the inconsistencies of behavior, the lack of control of impulses, the vagueness of thinking and the uncertainty of body identity which Anna Freud describes." Youngsters using marijuana tend to become easily confused, anxious, or depressed. They show poor social judgment and have trouble handling close relationships. Their attention span is short; they have difficulty concentrating and are often apathetic, passive, or indifferent. Deep inside, they develop feelings of hostility and distrust, while on the outside they may display exaggerated self-confidence. Many suffer a real sense of futility or hopelessness.

You must spell out clearly that marijuana is not for adolescents, but that you believe (were it legal) there should be a time limit on the ban, an age limit after which people could decide for themselves whether or not to use it. Stretching your attitude far enough to include the occasional social use of marijuana by adults, you put pot into a framework your children can more easily accept. Most young people are prepared to wait; waiting is something they understand. They have to wait for lots of things. Even when they do it grudgingly, they still do it. They are usually willing to wait until they get their licenses before they drive cars. When they don't, when they take off in the family station wagon or steal a car off the street, they are clearly acting out in self-destructive ways that have little to do with their need for wheels.

No matter what your drug attitude allows, there are very specific laws in this country about the use of marijuana. Pot-smoking youngsters are vulnerable to encounters with authority that can be even more damaging to them than the drug itself. By agreeing that marijuana might well be used occasionally by adults, you are not giving your youngster permission to light up the moment he turns eighteen. At that time, however, he will be legally responsible for himself. Hopefully, he will have acquired from you sound attitudes about the law, as well as about drugs, and if he believes that laws need changing, he will have some idea of how to go about effecting those changes.

The law in our country today is in such disrepute with many young people that some come close to believing there is merit in doing something that is against the law simply because it is against the law. The law is associated with the war in Vietnam, the shootings at Kent State and Jackson State, and the police riot during the 1968 Democratic convention in Chicago. Youngsters resent what has happened to their peers, harassed by police and arrested for a pinch of pot. Many of them see the law as directed against the nonestablished — the black, the poor, and the young.

though you may feel some sympathy for this point of view, it makes no sense for you to sound off angrily about "the pigs." Parents who condemn the police or the courts often deliver a message to their children that they do not really intend. They tell their young that the law is not a very useful social instrument and, in effect, give them permission to ignore the law, to disregard it, because some laws and some policemen are irrational, punitive, or wrong.

No youngster is going to respect *the law* unless he starts out by respecting *your law*. When he finds that your law is reasonable, and based on love and concern, he will form patterns of obedience and respect. He will follow your lead in dealing with authority. If he trusts you and you trust the law, then he will tend to trust it. This is not to suggest that you should indoctrinate your children with a mindless faith in authority. It would only set them up for the kind of disillusionment that shook up a whole generation in England at the time of Suez and in France during the Algerian crisis — and is now shaking up large numbers of young people in our country when they suddenly discover that their government can be immoral.

You must demonstrate to your child useful means of objecting to unjust laws, ways of working within political parties, voting, protesting, influencing legislators. In other words, he has to understand the political process as an instrument he can someday manipulate; he must see your hands on the levers, know that changes can be made and how they can be made.

Your attitude toward drugs and the law is not the only input your child receives. He gets information from school, television, and books, from newspapers, magazines, and the counterculture press, and from his friends. So your attitude may not prevail.

There are a number of complicated reasons why adolescents choose to use drugs. If we were to concentrate on one specific factor that seems intertwined with acting-out behavior in general and drug taking in particular, that factor would be sexuality.

Suddenly, during adolescence, a young person is able to function sexually — and is urged to do so. Internally, there is a wave of hormonal stimulation; externally, a barrage of psychological stimulation. Our culture seems to equate success as a man or a woman with sexual achievement, and adolescents are desperately concerned about establishing themselves in sexual roles. Anyone who practices any form of psychotherapy today is struck by this concern. Adolescents feel the need to try sex, to be sexually adult and competent, and to have successful heterosexual relationships, including intercourse. Yet they are frightened of rejection, failure, or impotence. Adolescents preparing for a date can be stricken to near paralysis by an emerging blemish or a skirt or shirt that doesn't fit. Their sexual trial runs are always intense and precarious ventures. Youngsters become even more vulnerable when parents inflict chinadoll attitudes on them, telling their daughters, for example, "You've got to save it until you are married." Such warnings only heighten the drama, increase the anxiety.

Young people have to go through a whole series of relationships in order to learn about themselves and about other people. They have to teach each other difficult lessons about giving and sharing. Eventually, they must master the cumbersome mechanics of sex.

Many young people reach out for drugs to help them with their sexual uncertainties. If they have been raised to believe in chemical solutions to most human problems, it is reasonable for them to expect some magical, chemical help now. And drugs do seem to help. Smoking marijuana with a date can increase intimacy and relax inhibitions. It does not create a *capacity* for intimacy where none exists, but it may provide the illusion of giving and sharing. Some youngsters find their anxieties sufficiently relieved to perform with sexual adequacy ile high, but the gain is illusory. Although marijuana may break down the barriers surrounding sexual activity, it only increases sexual uncertainty.

Many heroin addicts have had serious sexual problems in early adolescence. Boys were usually frightened of impotence or premature ejaculation, and early drug taking, specifically heroin taking, seemed to increase their sexual abilities. Heroin worked for them partly because they believed in the drug's magical properties, but mostly because of the tranquilizing effect of a small dose. In addition, there was some reduction in their perception of genital stimuli that allowed prolonged erections and ejaculations. But these sexual benefits were short-lived. Increased heroin use was accompanied by decreased sexual interest. In time, drug taking itself became the replacement for sex.

Youngsters rarely share sexual concerns with their parents. They shouldn't share them. Sexuality, with its special meanings and sensitivities, is best handled within the peer group, with others who are experiencing the same uncertainties. Young people must have this peer support; however, drugs and drug use are also a peer concern. Parents cannot control what goes on within this group, but there are ways they can keep tabs on it. They must reach out, and reach out carefully, because youngsters need to spend time away from their families while they are busy turning themselves into individuals, and parents can't interfere.

It is possible to dip into your children's peer group and sample the atmosphere there, not by invading the group's privacy, but by creating a setting, a place where you can periodically meet with your youngsters and their friends. This can be a bowling alley or a basketball court, a workshop or a garage. It isn't easy to find something to share with adolescents. Whatever you choose will be most effective if it lets you use some of your competencies. You might help them overhaul an engine

Dealing with Drugs 65

or caulk a boat, take them fishing or hunting, coach a team or lay out the school newspaper. One father, a mail clerk with no interest in music, became the manager of his son's rock band.

This kind of contact can become a very important forum. You may find your ideas challenged in ways your own child would never have dared to try alone. You will discover that youngsters can be tremendously open, anxious to talk about things that bother them, about school and families, sexuality and politics, and about drugs. The drug talk will come easily if you don't turn it off. It will come because other parents *have* turned it off.

You will get a standard set of drug apologetics: "There's nothing wrong with drug taking . . . Adults take drugs too . . . They take alcohol . . . They take pills. What's wrong with kids taking *their* drugs? After all, drugs don't hurt anybody. Alcohol hurts people, causes crimes and violence and bloody accidents. We aren't doing anything that adults don't do, and it is pure hypocrisy for them to lay prohibitions on us while they themselves are so deeply involved in drugs."

The young are not ignorant. They know that "speed" kills, and many are still concerned about possible chromosomal damage caused by acid (LSD). Their biggest chunk of misinformation is the general conviction that marijuana is a "safe" drug. They argue that there is no evidence yet to indicate physical danger — but they miss, or perhaps ignore, the strong evidence of psychological danger.

Once you've started this group, you should be prepared for what you are going to hear. Your attitude toward drugs is reasonable and logical, and you can hold firmly to it without having to beat the kids down or shut them up. You must be willing to repeat yourself, to use various analogies, to accept every valid argument they raise and not get stuck in ridiculous positions, such as trying to defend the misuse of alcohol.

It will help if you are willing to expose yourself as a fallible human being, who has made mistakes and lost control on occasion. You may not have taken drugs, but you have drunk too much or driven too fast, and sharing the humiliation or the embarrassment of these situations goes a long way toward making what you say, as a parent, meaningful and real.

Don't expect to *win* these discussions. Hold your ground even if you don't have the youngsters "crying uncle." Let them walk away from the talk without the humiliation of having to say, "You're right," or, "We give up." There's no triumph if they concede and stop talking. They have to test what you say, try it on and see how it fits in their lives.

Working with this group, you can demonstrate to your own child how to deal with conflicting points of view. Being reasonable, decent, friendly, and open and yet not being swayed, you show him you can maintain a relationship in spite of opposing views. This is important, for kids often have an "all or nothing" feeling. They believe that if someone opposes them, if he takes a position different from theirs, the relationship is wiped out. You can reveal something quite different; your child will bring away from these talks the reassuring idea that there are times when differences can actually bring people closer together.

There may be youngsters in the group who have already begun using drugs, but are taking them with a great deal of anxiety. They are beginning to recognize that it doesn't feel right. It's like driving a car too fast — exciting but a little frightening. If what you say clarifies those feelings, you'll develop secret allies who may not speak up then, but will come around later and admit, "You know, what you said made a lot of sense."

There's a good chance your child will feel the need to find out about drugs for himself, to check you out. What you hope is that he will perform his research within the margins of safety and that the experiment won't fill a dramatic need for vengeance or repudiation. (This is not likely to be the case if you have done even part of your job well.) If he plays it safe and gets high on pot once or twice and finds that it is no big thing, then he has satisfied his curiosity about drugs.

He may even yield to the pressure of his peers, accept their demand that he try what they have been doing, test their assertion that it provides greater intimacy and camaraderie. Youngsters sometimes feel the need to undergo this kind of initiation before they are free to reject the group's notions or break away from the group itself.

You are not likely to discover your youngster's experiment. There is no reason you need know about it. But should you stumble upon some indicator — a roach (marijuana cigarette butt) or a small bag of grass — should you smell the distinctively sweet smell of pot out in the garage, take it as a warning and be alert for further signs of drug use.

How can you tell if your child is taking drugs? There are no sure proofs, except finding the drugs or finding the child taking drugs or coming upon him when he is high or low or way out somewhere. It may be useful to know that psychoactive drugs may cause a general sluggishness, poor comprehension, and slow speech; they can bring on jitters, loss of appetite, and heavy perspiration. Poor complexion, acne, and itching are signs of drug use. But youngsters are aware of these signs. They know lots of pot can make their eyes red, and they may use an eyewash before they come home for inspection.

Instead of looking for drugs, or symptoms of drug use, look for changes in the youngster himself. Is he keeping peculiar hours? Has his schoolwork suddenly gone bad? Has he lost weight? Has his dress changed from casual to sloppy to downright dirty? Is he often vague and withdrawn? Many of these signs, like frequent changes of mood, are typical of all adolescents at one time or another. Their need for privacy may lead them to secret ways, furtive phone calls and meetings that have nothing to do with drugs. However, if you know your child and you have caught on to a combination of these changes, then you have good reasons for making a move.

The situation becomes urgent when, having noticed some of this peculiar behavior by your child, you find a second indicator, such as a roach in the ashtray of your car. Understand that for every joint you spot there have possibly been another ten, twenty, or more. You are studying the tiniest tip of the iceberg, and the time has come to act directly.

Don't confront your child at the moment of discovery. You will probably be too angry or worried. If he is still under the influence of whatever drug he has taken, it makes no more sense to talk to him than to argue with a drunk. You need time, not ten minutes before you leave for work or half an hour before you're due at an evening meeting, but a chunk of time that can be isolated. And this talk may just be the opening session of a whole series of talks lasting several weeks. There is no need to rush to judgment or take any short cuts toward where you are going. But it is important to *know* where you are going, that you are heading straight toward a demand, a fiat, an ultimatum: NO DRUGS, capital letters and underlined.

You begin by telling your child what you have noticed, what you have found, how he has changed, and that you are very concerned. Then you give him an opening so that he can begin to talk and present his side. He is going to be feeling enough guilt and probably a good deal of relief that you have brought up the subject, so that he will try to right the score and will talk freely if you let him.

You might be lucky. Your child may have already reached the point where he believes he has been through it and drug use is actually over for him. That's great if it's true. It is also one way to get you off his back. The common way is to lie, to deny using drugs. If he does admit it, he will usually admit only part of the truth, insisting that he is a step down from where he really is. Should your child stick with complete denial in the face of your certainty, if he refuses to accept that you *know*, then you may have gotten there too late. His druggism may already be established.

Most youngsters will eventually own up to at least part of what they have been doing. When your child begins to talk, you should hear out all his reasons and rationalizations, keeping in mind your own position, your own attitude, and your own commitment to end this talk or series of talks by laying down the law — no drugs.

Many parents cannot stand convincingly behind this demand. They do not understand that they must be prepared to do literally *anything* to stop their youngster from using drugs. Parents have gone through the most degrading and frightening experiences before finally coming to accept this position. If a parent knows that he is willing to commit a child, through the courts, to a treatment program or a state institution, that he is willing, at bottom line, to put his child out of the house and stop supporting him, that he will do all these things to enforce his demand, then he can make the demand, "No drugs," out of real belief and not as an hysterical outburst.

You don't have to spell out the limits to which you are prepared to go in order to make your demand stick. Your youngster can probably tell how strong your commitment is and, in many cases, that is all he needs. He has, in fact, been waiting for you to act. All the little clues you found could well have been his red flags, his distress signals, alerting you to his need, his fear of losing control. He may also have been telling you that there was some lack of concern or support at home, and this should be speedily remedied if you want to avoid a replay of the drug discovery and confrontation drama.

Even if your youngster is relieved that you have stepped in and taken hold, he isn't going to show that by crying, "God bless you, Daddy, you really care." Inside he can be unwind-

mad, but up on the surface he will show anger at your ...erence, resentment at your mistrust, and embarrassment ... the whole situation. Replying firmly and calmly to his anger, you can nail down more firmly your position of *no drugs*.

Parents are often overly concerned about what substances their children are using. They try to divide psychoactives into hard and soft drugs, assuming that there is some kind of difference in the drug-using process that depends upon the particular brand involved. These are unreal distinctions. Druggism works the same way with all drugs. A heroin user has probably used some other drug regularly and moved to heroin when he found his initial drug of choice was insufficient for his needs.

There is also considerable parental concern about *treating* their children when they come home, or are delivered home, while still under the influence of a psychoactive drug. The rule for this is simple. Any time your youngster is out of control, seems out of his mind or in a stupor, he should be seen by a doctor. He should also be examined by a doctor if you believe he has been using heroin. Most parents have had no experience locating needle marks or recognizing tracks (the depressed or inflamed veins that mark narcotic addicts).

There is a limit to the amount of druggism that you, as a parent, can handle yourself. If your youngster violates your antidrug injunction, if he is already dependent on a drug or if he is using heroin, you have more than you can handle alone, and it is time to go for help.

Before reaching your own limit, you should check out the resources available in your community, learn what the schools, churches, mental health clinics, hospitals, and private social agencies are doing about drugs. Many cities and some good-sized towns now have self-help groups, run by trained ex-addicts or drug-wise counselors, that work with drug-troubled young people. Your child now needs this help, because he isn't getting enough of what he must have from you and can't handle his druggism alone. He needs the support of peers within the group, the demands of the group, and a chance to explore *all* the feelings that have gotten him where he is now. It may not be possible for him to share these feelings with his parents.

How do you get your youngster into such a group if he is unwilling to go? By following through on your earlier commitment to do *anything* necessary to stop him from using drugs. You can even use the courts to enforce your demand. Juvenile authorities will often go along with parents seriously concerned with helping their child. Should the court require your child to attend a self-help group, it can back up that requirement with far less attractive alternatives, such as youth shelters and state institutions. If your youngster is old enough, you can threaten to turn him out of the house. And if he doesn't comply with your demand, that is exactly what you must do.

If you continue to keep your child at home, feeding him, clothing him, and making no effort to stop his drug use, except to "insist" ineffectually that he give it up, then you are supporting his druggism. You are helping him to be sick. Chicken soup and sympathy are no remedies for druggism. Drug dependency is, in many ways, pleasant. Drug users *like* using drugs. They will only stop when drug use becomes *unpleasant,* and this takes a long time. It is an ugly, sordid process that can destroy your child. You can't wait until he is ready to get better. You have to make his drug use unpleasant enough *now,* so that he will want to recover.

Once your youngster is in a self-help group, any number of things can happen. He may get just the kind of support he needs, drop his drugs, work out his other problems, and get himself together. It may be useful for you to get some help too, from either the group or some other source. Your child still lives at home. Whatever condition made it impossible for you to prevent his druggism still exists. You haven't turned over your job as parent to the group. You have asked for help, and it is possible that you need some of that help for yourself.

If a really full-blown case of druggism exists, the self-help group is not likely to arrest it. What your child needs is something more intense, more highly structured, such as a therapeutic community.

But before looking at the way a therapeutic community works, let's try to deal with some of the questions parents will have about the suggestions in this chapter.

How can I stop my son from using marijuana when he sees nothing wrong with it, when his friends and many of their parents see nothing wrong with it?

By *telling* him to stop it. Your son is breaking the law. No matter what you or he thinks about the law, he is putting himself in considerable jeopardy.

An adolescent who is getting high muddles his thinking about things that are quite difficult for him to deal with — his parents, his girl, his friends, where he is going, and what will besome of him. He may get some relief from this generalized worry and anxiety by smoking marijuana, but this will eventually increase his sense of helplessness.

His rationale, that he and his friends and some of their parents see nothing wrong with smoking marijuana, is a very thin veneer. If you don't let yourself be bullied by this pseudosociologic bravado, you can get him to think about the real reasons he is using grass. He will discover that it isn't just to feel good or because it is exciting, but because there are things he is worried about, that confuse him. Smoking grass is not going to help that. It will only make him continue to feel like a kid.

Isn't a flat demand like "no drugs" too heavy to suddenly impose on a child?

You have to rid yourself of the notion that your child is a precious piece of pottery who is going to break apart when

Dealing with Drugs 73

you tell him to stop whatever he is doing. If you make some clear demands and set some limits, he will probably follow them. He'll do it because, if there's been anything sound in your relationship, your child still wants to please you and wants you to have a high regard for him.

The converse is also true. If your youngster gets away with murder, if you take a helpless position and give him license to violate what you deem important, then he feels, in some ways, that he is violating himself. He feels bad about himself and worse about you. There is a real sense of despair.

Shouldn't adolescents be allowed to make choices for themselves?

Your child should have no choice to make about using drugs. You make that choice for him. When he is independent in the world and can write his own ticket and live under his own roof, when he can support himself emotionally, vocationally, and in all other ways, then he can make a choice.

He may choose not to follow your demands. He may decide, when he is sixteen or seventeen, that he doesn't like Father's rule anymore and he is going to leave. If, on the other hand, you allow him to do anything he wants while you are still supporting him, giving him permission to ignore everything you supposedly believe in, you assume an attitude of no attitude, a position of no position. And your child ends up with no position too, because he has no one to challenge, no way he can firm up what he believes. He is fighting with a straw man, throwing punches into putty.

Won't these demands destroy my relationship with my child?

You should be worrying about your child and not your relationship with him.

There is a purpose to childhood — learning how to live successfully in the adult world. The parental relationship is not an end in itself but a way of preparing youngsters to have relationships with other people. Sometimes parents lose sight of this and become overly concerned about their own relationship with their children. This makes it difficult for them to make demands, because they cannot risk being the bad guy, the demanding guy. They begin to treat their children as peers, as colleagues, as friends. But children are *not* your equals; they are neither your peers nor your friends. If you have your children as friends later in life, it will be because you have managed to keep an appropriate parental distance along the way.

Is there something wrong in wanting your children to like you?

Your children should like you. But you can't let your desire to be liked interfere with your position as a parent, with your responsibilities to your child. Somehow parents have gotten the idea, perhaps from advertising or politics, that everything in life must have a candy coating. Everything has to taste good. But not everything can taste good. It is unpleasant — but necessary — for your son to find out that he can't do everything he wants to do. He cannot live in your house and mess the place up, or trade drugs, or smoke pot. He can't do that — unless you let him.

How does a parent deal with the troubles underlying drug use?

You have to deal with what is presented to you, what is apparent. You can't try to be a psychoanalyst. You are the boss of your family system, and your responsibility includes dealing with violations, making children accountable for what they are doing within that system. When you meet that responsibility, you put yourself into position to take the next step.

If your child can't smoke grass to burn his worries away and his anxieties are no longer going up in smoke, you may find he

Dealing with Drugs 75

will come to you and begin to talk about some of the things that are concerning him.

Won't my "no drug" demand cut my child off from his friends?

At times, the price of integrity is loneliness.

You can't create a magical, artificial atmosphere for your child and expect him to grow to deal with reality. In fact, you will prevent him from growing by giving him, or allowing him, unreal solutions. Your task as a parent is to help him see the world more clearly and not to perpetuate his infantile notions of self-importance.

Can't I make different rules for my child, who is really quite special?

It is cruel to encourage a myth of "specialness" that includes a kind of infantile entitlement to have whatever he wants, whenever he wants it. Any time a parent wants to be much more understanding of his child, much more accommodating than his parents were with him, he prevents his child from learning about the world as he learned about it. He is in danger of committing the worst developmental crime of all, removing the confrontation with reality that children need in order to grow up. The task of childhood is to grow up and make it in the real world, not to dwell in the make-believe world that good Father wants to maintain for his magic prince or princess.

How often do parents actually have to follow through and throw their children out?

Parents rarely have to go that far, but being ready to do it is what drives your message home and makes your child come around and say, "Okay, I'll go by the rules." He may turn to his friends and tell them, "You know, my old man is a son of a bitch. You know what he did? He really clamped the irons on me." Actually, though, your stern requirements are going to make him feel very safe.

How can a sixteen-year-old make it, if he is thrown out of his home?

With great difficulty, if at all. But the shock of realizing his dependency is exactly what he needs to face the fact that as long as he lives in your house, he has to obey you. If the situation has come this far, your child is quite puffed up with his own smoke, and he really believes that he'll be able to get away with whatever he wants. You have to deflate him.

Most kids who are tossed out only spend a night or two away from home. But the effect on the child of that painful experience — going out the door and realizing what he is leaving and not wanting to leave it — is powerful. When he returns, the balance of power changes, and you are back in control.

Sometimes a youngster finds a place to stay for a while, but he soon gets in touch with his family for money, clothes, or food. Parents usually want to supply these things, because they feel uncomfortable about what they have done. Yet if they stick to their resolve, they have a better chance of bringing their child back home and under home rule.

7. The Phoenix Way

SOME FIFTY MILES north of New York City, at the end of a long, green valley, is a farm where about fifty young people live. There are cows and horses, dogs and cats, and a kitchen garden. The old buildings have been scrubbed and painted, whitewashed rocks mark the road, and there is a general bustle and atmosphere of purpose to the place. Some of the youngsters seem shy, yet most smile and stick out their hands when a stranger arrives. They introduce themselves, and hurry off to find whomever you ask to meet. By then, you have already seen a good part of what you are curious about. All the young people there were heavily into drugs or addicted when they arrived, and it is these young people that you have come to see.

The Putnam Valley farm is part of Phoenix House, the nation's largest therapeutic community for the treatment of druggism. Most of the youngsters who come there, who need the highly structured environment of such a community, have passed the point where the intervention of their parents, even with the support of self-help groups, can break them loose from drugs. Typical of these young people, many of whom have dramatic histories of drug abuse, are Michael, Suzanne, Darryl, and Dennis, four of the current residents.

Michael is sixteen. When he was two, his father left home. His mother moved the family from New Jersey to Manhattan's East Harlem and went on welfare. Michael started smoking marijuana when he was ten, snorting heroin at thirteen, and shooting the year after. In junior high school, his habit was costing ten to twelve dollars a day. He stole from the school, broke into a few stores, snatched purses. His formal education stopped on his fifth day in high school, and after that he was on the street for eight months.

"I always thought my mother knew," he says, "but she was afraid to say anything. I'd come home high, and she'd say, 'You're probably drunk.'" But one day, his older brother began to question Michael about the long-sleeved shirt he wore to hide his tracks. "I'd even sleep in that shirt. And my brother, he told me to show him my arms. My mother came in and said I had to show her too. I ran out of the house, trying to get away from my mother. I thought she was going to kill me."

Badly shaken, Michael ran to a place he had heard about, where many drug-troubled young people in New York City go for help. He ran to a Phoenix Center, first stop on the way to Phoenix House. That day, when his mother frightened him, it suddenly became important for Michael to do something about his drug use. Yet that night the crisis passed. The pressure was off. "My mother told me she was only playing with me." The next day, when Michael let the center director know he wouldn't be coming back, "He told me he'd call my mother and tell her I was a dope fiend." So, Michael stuck it out; he began putting in several hours a day at the center. His mother believed he had taken a job.

The staff at the center, ex-addict residents of Phoenix House, worked with Michael, molding his fears about drugs, his anxieties about what was happening to him, into a real resolve to recover. Youngsters must prove their resolve before they move into one of Phoenix's fifteen residences. They have to show up every day, be honest in group discussions, and kick their habit, so that they can come in clean. Many aren't able to stay drug-free; sometimes medically aided detoxification is necessary for young people whose desire to get better isn't yet matched by the responsibility to do *everything* they must.

When Michael was ready to go to Phoenix, he wasn't really clean. "I'd kicked for two days, but I couldn't stay off. I was still getting high at night." He wasn't worried about that. He was worried about his mother's finally learning of his addiction. When the director told her, "She said she'd suspected. But she was afraid of what people would say, that nobody would talk to her. But she was glad I was going."

Suzanne has just turned seventeen. There is something strong and clean about her scrubbed face and bleached blue jeans and the straightforward way she tells of her problem past. Her parents separated when she was thirteen and already well into amphetamines. "I used to steal diet pills." Living with her grandmother after the divorce, she moved up from marijuana and amphetamines to LSD. "My grandmother knew I was taking drugs. She kept pleading, 'Don't get high.' " But Suzanne kept getting high. She was failing at school, stopped going, and finally ran away to California. Picked up by police in Los Angeles, she was shipped back to her father in New Jersey. A private mental hospital was his answer to Suzanne's problems. There, "They filled me full of Thorazine," and she boasts about how she "had people bringing in dope and was switching pills with the old ladies."

After her release, Suzanne went back to her grandmother and back to drugs. She was now using both LSD and heroin and took her last trip in an empty parking lot, where police found her "totally out of it." Doctors at a youth shelter discovered she had hepatitis, and a nurse there told her about Phoenix. Her father agreed to that solution and she was admitted about one year ago.

Darryl, also seventeen, a tall, angular boy, is still slightly awed by his garish history. His parents were divorced when he was three. At eleven he was smoking marijuana: "Everybody was smoking pot." But two years later, Darryl moved past pot and hashish to amphetamines. "After that it was more acid and less speed." He had been seeing a psychotherapist since he was nine. "My therapist knew I was taking drugs. When I was thirteen, she threatened to tell my father, and after that I didn't tell her nothing."

Darryl was fourteen and living in San Francisco with his mother when his druggism became apparent. His schoolwork fell apart. "I lost interest in everything." He left home, moved into Haight-Ashbury, and finally was sent to his father in New York. "My father was told I was taking drugs. He accepted it. He didn't know I was going crazy with drugs."

His father sent him to a boarding school, then a ranch in Montana, then a mental hospital. After that, Darryl ran away again and was living in New York's East Village, "using needles, shooting LSD," until he got hepatitis. When he was released from the hospital, he went to live in a small upstate town with his mother, "But I got busted for turning kids on in the junior high school." His next stop, another boarding school, worked for a while. Darryl stayed clean and finished ninth grade.

Back in New York that summer, he was mixed up with drugs again, selling heroin and experimenting with cocaine. When he was picked up by the police, Darryl had two thousand dollars in cash, three joints of marijuana, and a drop of cocaine on him. Expecting nothing more serious than probation when his case came to court, he started dealing again. "Until one day I went to court and they sprang it on me — go to Phoenix House."

Darryl's father had overruled his lawyer and convinced the court to take a hard line with his son, to place the boy in Phoenix House. He gave Darryl no warning. "He finally realized he was going to have to play the game my way — sneaky, treacherous, deceitful. He said I could go in for three months. But after three months, I realized I was still pretty messed up in my head." It's almost a year now, and Darryl is much less messed up.

Dennis didn't have Darryl's advantages. Nor did he have

his varied pharmacological experience. When he was fourteen he was using heroin, as were most of his eighth grade class and most of his brothers and sisters. There were no experiments with marijuana or pills; Dennis went straight to smack — right to heroin. His experiences were different because Central Harlem is different. His parents were together and when they learned about their son (after six months) they regularly brought him to family court. Just as regularly, Dennis would promise to attend a Phoenix Center and instead head straight for the street. It took almost a year, but his parents kept the pressure on and he finally entered Phoenix. He is sixteen now and has been a resident for seven months. Some of his shyness and distrust still remain, but most has been worn away.

Michael, Suzanne, Darryl, and Dennis are on their way back. Stopping drugs was only the first step. Michael had to learn that he counts, that he is important, Suzanne to give and accept love, Darryl to abandon his adolescent notions of grandiosity, and Dennis to trust and to be trusted. Each of them, like all youngsters in therapeutic communities, is in the process of growing up, going through the adolescence their druggism denied them.

The growing up is the cure, for until these youngsters are full, complete, and functional adults they remain vulnerable to drugs. That is why druggism is so hard to shake loose once it takes hold. It replaces normal life. It is a way of life itself.

From interviews conducted by sociologist Henry L. Lennard with long-time drug users at Phoenix, two major differences between the "straight" and drug style of life are apparent.

(1) *The veteran drug user is a true loner.*

"You don't want anybody else, because you don't trust nobody. The less people you deal with, the better."

"I existed within a six-block radius. That's the only place I felt secure."

"When I was dealing drugs, the guy I got the stuff from brought it to my room. I stayed in that room, with a bed and a TV and a radio and about two thousand magazines, and I never went out for three and a half months. If I wanted food, I'd send out for it. I didn't want to leave. I had everything I needed."

(2) *All activity is involved with getting and using drugs.*

"You cop, go home and shoot up, nod for a while, go out and hustle some bread to cop again. Nothing happens except somebody gets busted or dies. And you don't care unless it's your dealer."

"To me, going to a party was a drag. I'd just nod out, and nine times out of ten I'd be asked to leave anyway, because I'd burned something up with a cigarette."

"You know, the dope fiend never talks about nothing. They're the most tight-lipped individuals; nothing ever goes wrong. Nothing! Everything is always fine. Only thing that ever goes wrong is if you don't have no money to cop."

Even among addicts who cop (buy) and shoot together there is little real communication. Lennard concluded that they "develop a practiced disregard for each other's feelings and situations."

Parents often imagine that druggism is like measles or whooping cough, that it can be treated specifically until the symptoms go away, that their child can continue to live at home, go to school, see his friends, do all the things he was doing while he was using drugs. He can't. If his druggism is already established, it is well protected by his attitudes, his way of life, his circle of drugmates. He has created for himself or fallen into an area of such contagion that he will constantly reinfect himself until he is taken out of it.

Traditional psychiatry has no answer for drug abuse. "Individual psychotherapy has shown itself to be incapable of interrupting a pattern of drug dependence in significant numbers of patients," writes Dr. Matthew P. Dumont in *The American Handbook of Psychiatry,* and most psychiatrists will admit that they have few means to stop patients from doing what gives them pleasure, no matter how harmful it may be. The treatment available in programs of civil commitment for addicts and in most mental hospitals rarely works, because nothing changes very much for the patients. They have been plucked from environments that offer no way out of drugs and placed in others that allow them no way to grow. They emerge from these institutions the same drug-prone types that entered, momentarily clean but unlikely to remain that way. Drugs were taken away and nothing replaced them.

Methadone maintenance of narcotic addicts, unavailable to anyone under eighteen, does indeed replace the drug — with a synthetic narcotic just as addicting. Advocates of methadone programs believe they will reduce the amount of addict crime by supplying a free substitute for heroin (and some critics now suggest going all the way and supplying the heroin itself). Methadone by itself, however, does not change the addict's way of life, nor does it prevent him from using other, nonnarcotic drugs. It is not a solution any parent is likely to choose for his child. It is not a cure for druggism.

To fight their way free from drugs and druggism, youngsters need a place where they can break through their walls of silence and suspicion, so they can grow into new ways of dealing with the world, learn responsible ways to regard themselves. This is what a family should do. But when the family, for whatever reason, has failed, then the youngster must have another kind of family. Therapeutic communities are families, communities of young and old with a shared experience of drug use. Within such families, young people can learn or relearn openness and honesty and serve a kind of emotional apprenticeship under those who have gone the route from down-and-out druggism to leadership within the community.

The first therapeutic community, Synanon, was started at Santa Monica in 1958. Today, communities are open or about to open in cities all over the country. Ideally, there will someday be a network of self-help groups and therapeutic communities linked together and touching every part of the country. Meanwhile, there are still places in the nation where no such facilities exist, where the needs of drug-troubled families are not being properly met. Where therapeutic communities do exist, some are stronger and more effective than others, for standards of treatment have not yet been established, and much of any community's strength depends upon the training of its ex-addict staff.

Phoenix House, which has trained staff members for communities all over the country, has more than 1200 residents in fourteen houses within New York City, plus the Putnam Valley farm. First conceived as a program for adult addicts, Phoenix has shifted its concern as its population changed. Now half the new residents are teen-agers and the youngest member is eight.

There is a Phoenix Center near each residence, and most youngsters who make it into the program are brought to one of these centers by their parents. Parents who have mishandled their child's druggism often wake up to the seriousness of his problem when the symptoms become acute, or their youngster is arrested. They work with the center staff and keep the pressure on their child. Other parents fight the problem and the program, shocked or ashamed when they learn their child has come to Phoenix for help. These parents insist that their children are not deeply involved with drugs. "She's just experimenting," one mother maintained. "She's lying to you. She tells me the truth, and she's only been at it a couple of months." But center workers, who were copping and shooting when the current Phoenix candidates were stealing Daddy's Dexedrine, can easily spot a serious drug problem. That mother's daughter had been using drugs regularly for more than two years. Somehow, the mother believed she could make it all better, and told the girl, "I don't want anybody to know. I'll get you a private doctor. I'll fix it for you." It was too shameful, too embarrassing for her to have her daughter in treatment. It was easier to go on living with a junkie child.

Youngsters moving into a Phoenix House are wary. They are frightened. A girl leaving the center to become a resident, holding her suitcase, with a big kiss from the center director for luck, is close to tears. A boy whose only choice was Phoenix or jail comes in tight and angry, burying his hostility as the girl buries her terror. They find their new home scrubbed clean and neat, maddeningly orderly after their years of disorder. They soon learn what their new "family" expects of them: first, *no drugs* and *no violence*. They're supposed to make their beds, take showers, and obey orders. They catch on quickly that their druggy ways are unacceptable. They can't lie, they can't cheat, they can't goof off or withdraw. They aren't going to be coddled, and they aren't going to be protected. They *are* going to be helped, supported, and even loved, although it takes them time to recognize and accept this.

The Phoenix family works, as all families work, only when care and concern are constant. The door is always open. Anybody can leave. There are no locks or bars or guards. Youngsters stay because they learn they have to stay, that they need what the community can give them, and they want the emotional warmth they can share there.

Mark, who is now sixteen and lives at the house on Manhattan's West 85th Street, where the community began, remembers, "I didn't want to stay. That was more than a year ago. But after a while I got comfortable. I had friends. Like I never had any real friends, no back coverage like this on the street. Here, somebody always looks out for you. When you're down, there's always someone to help you up. It doesn't happen all at once. I took a little time to put trust in people. But when somebody tells you what he wouldn't tell other people, then you give him something back."

Each house, like any family group, has its "parents" — the director and two assistant directors, the only resident staff — most of whom are former addicts and Phoenix graduates. One of the top three in each house is always a woman. They are models for the new arrival, for each of them once stood where he now stands. Others who serve as examples are the family's older brothers and sisters, long-term residents — "the strength of the house" — who carry major responsibility within the community.

Under the staff is an entire resident hierarchy, topped by department supervisors, with section heads, trouble-shooters, and workers. They run the house, cook and serve, clean and repair, keep records, greet visitors, and buy supplies. Every resident has a job and a rank and his status is never in doubt. Elaborate organization charts are common. Residents are urged to "seek and assume" responsibility, to go after the jobs they want. Promotion is based on progress in the program, how well the aspirant is learning to handle himself, as well as performance on the job.

Newcomers are not in line for promotions; nor are they permitted to go out unaccompanied. They have no visitors, make no phone calls, send no letters. The break with the past must be total and abrupt. "It's like growing up all over again," Mark explains. "When your mother grew you up, she taught you how to walk. When you could walk and when you could take care of yourself, she sent you to school. When she got trust in you, she let you go."

During their first nine months, new residents rarely leave the house alone. They may go in groups or accompanied by an older resident. When they get that first pass, when they are out on their own for the first time, they usually head back to their old turf to find there is nothing there for them. "You feel protected here. You can't wait to get out, but after a while, you can't wait to get back. I hit the corner and run all the way back to the house."

Like most families, Phoenix has punishments as well as rewards. There are tough dressing-downs, called "haircuts," and there are literal haircuts, shaved heads for truly grave offenses like running away. Youngsters who walk through the open door usually come back and have to take their medicine — a shaved head for a boy or a stocking cap for a girl, and twelve or sixteen hours on a hard bench by the doorway. Other offenses may be punished by loss of privileges, or chores like shining every shoe in the house. Sometimes the humiliation is small — wearing a sign that reads I'M A THIEF. DON'T TRUST ME, or I'M A BABY. PLEASE HELP ME. The idea is that anyone who misbehaves is indeed a baby. Residents can be demoted as well as promoted, and it is common for them to lose their first big job, becoming puffed-up and self-important and winding up "back in the dishpan" on the kitchen staff or scrubbing out the toilets. Status is real at Phoenix because it is constantly earned and easily lost. Dignity is learned through the system of rewards, punishment, and humiliation.

Phoenix is a busy place. No one lounges around the house, few residents watch much television, and there is little time to play cards. Up to seven, they breakfast by eight and are at work until lunch. There are seminars in the afternoon, group discussions, guest speakers, debates. Druggism has been so consuming a life that many new residents are just not in touch with what is going on in the world. Seminars help to make them aware and help them overcome the shyness and inarticulateness that is common to drug users. Classes for younger residents keep them up to grade level so that they can resume school when they are ready, while older residents work for their high school equivalency.

By the time residents are ready to move up to the next step

— preparing to leave — they have become responsible senior members, the strength of the house, and have a special status. Many leave the house each day to work or attend school or for special job training. Some start preparing to take staff jobs at Phoenix or with similar programs.

The Phoenix family, with its hierarchy and promotions, its rewards and demands, would blow apart if there were not some way to deal with anger and hostility. Prohibitions against drugs and violence bar the ways in which most residents once acted out. In fact, all kinds of wholesome behavior are demanded of them. Where, then, do these strong feelings come out? They come out in the encounter. In many ways, encounters are what Phoenix provides in place of drugs. They are intense, emotional, and explosive. They are high dramas with ceremonial aspects. Many participants bring to them all the pleasantly fearful anticipations they once brought to drugs. But encounters are a way of growing; they are the main means of moving residents toward the independence and maturity they need to leave Phoenix as whole individuals.

Encounters and encounter-like groups are common outside therapeutic communities. Many psychotherapists use them to help "straight" people clear away the emotional debris that prevents them from acting or feeling or being the way they want to act or feel or be. The Phoenix encounter is more of a battle than these civilian models. The group is more likely to attack and indict members, because it is harder to break through the heavy defenses of addicts and other drug users. Often the group must generate guilts and anxieties in a member, for these are the engines of change, but many residents aren't yet open enough to let loose their own guilts or anxieties. Attacks at Phoenix are directed against anything antisocial, amoral, self-defeating, or immature, anything that is deemed ignorant or "stupid behavior."

Beginners, who aren't ready to learn from encounters, must learn about them and how to use them. They shout and curse,

The Phoenix Way

getting out raw feelings without gaining much insight. But they soon see that "dumping the garbage in their guts" makes them feel better. They understand that they can yell and be yelled at and that anything goes, anything can be said, and no one gets hurt. The distinctions of rank and status are dropped during encounters. The rawest new resident can berate the house director if he chooses, let his resentments loose at his superiors.

As residents learn about encounters, they bring more understanding to them, develop insights into their own lives and use these insights to help others.

Encounters aren't haphazard. They move along a line determined by the leader. Action starts with an indictment against someone in the group, who becomes the focus. The group then moves in, pulling pieces of information from the subject until there is enough to understand his behavior. By overstatement and caricature, with insults and goading, the group urges the subject to blow off his feelings while defending himself against the charges. These defenses usually complete the "fabric of behavior" the group has created.

A girl who has been playing coy, sexy games is condemned by the group as "whore" and "tramp," who will "ball anything that walks." Magnifying her offenses, they force her to really look at how she devalues her body and devalues herself. Meanwhile, somewhere else in the house, the boys who played along with her games are catching it for the dishonest and irresponsible way they dealt with her.

In spite of the street language, the cursing and crudeness, there is an overwhelming sense of concern within the group. This love is often expressed brutally and crudely but it is always there. Without it, the encounter wouldn't work. Statements are exaggerated but feelings are real — the tears and anger, love and concern.

Once the subject "cops to" the indictment, when he understands and accepts the group's formulation of where he is and what he is, he is committed to change. The group extracts a "contract" for a specific piece of behavior. A resident who is always late, and has come to see some of his problems with authority, may be put on contract to be five minutes early during the next two weeks. The contract is a reminder of the real problem and his need to deal with it. Also, by "practicing the form," residents claim, "you achieve the essence." As he stops behaving as though he resents authority, he will begin to stop resenting it.

Sometimes there are special encounters. A group of younger residents might get together, occasionally an all-girl group is held, and long-time residents meet to deal with the problems they face preparing to leave the house. Veteran residents are old hands at the "game." They close in quickly on a problem and are open and vulnerable when focused upon.

The following vignettes were part of a senior residents' encounter at the Phoenix House on 116th Street in Manhattan.

(First into focus was Mike, who holds an important job in the house but still has troubles caused by his delayed adolescence.)

Others: (*To Mike*) About two days ago, there were a couple of guys in my room, enjoying themselves, playing records. And you came in and cussed us out. You put on such a fucking scene, it was unbelievable. Then, you go back to your room and start knocking down the walls. And I came over to see you, and you cussed me out again. And I want to know what the fuck is going on with you.

Mike: (*Calmly*) It was one-thirty in the morning, Sunday morning, and you were playing records. I banged on the wall, and the records just got louder. I never heard a record play so loud.

(*Mike's attacker and he start to shout at each other about who is to blame and who is lying.*)

Others: That's not the point. It's the people you claim you're so overjoyed about having as friends, that you can come and talk to any time you want. What about them? What kind of an attitude is that to take?

It's not the fucking record player, it's your attitude.

(The group pours on the criticism until Mike admits he made a mistake.)

Mike: I know. I'll straighten it out. I came out a little sideways.

(Mike's excuse for his short temper is the trouble he has been having on the job. He feels he is given a hard time, that he isn't trusted. Most recently, he was criticized for taking a girl with him when he left the house on business. The girl, whom he had known when he was on drugs, is now a resident. Mike had been warned to stay away from her. But he excuses himself: "They only said not to hang out with her too tough."

The rest of the group is certain Mike lets his social life get in the way of his responsibilities. He denies this, insists the real trouble is that no one trusts him.)

Mike: *(Referring to a time he was sent to buy something and returned without it)* They started yelling *(he shouts),* "You don't have the money. We know you don't have the money. You spent it." I said I got the money. It was in the petty-cash box. "We don't believe you," they said. And I had to go and get the money and show them. And it makes me feel like shit.

(The others remind him that he has been careless with money before. They keep after him. "It's your

attitude," they insist, and go back to the phonograph incident.)

Others: You're one of the strengths of the house, and there's a roomful of young ones next door. And in front of them, you shout, "Shut the fuck up. Get the fuck out of my room. You want to fight?"

You're impulsive. You go right over the edge. Even after something happens, you don't think or feel if anyone got hurt in the process.

When you don't win an argument, it's the end of the world. Off you go.

Leader: Do you accept any of this?
Mike: Yeah, I do. I get angry sometimes, and I know I came out sounding on George.
Leader: The more uptight you get, the more erratic you become, the more there are going to be people who think they've got to make decisions for you. And they are going to keep telling you what to do. And it's because you're not thinking.

(Sometime later, the focus switched to Willy, not a regular member of the group, who had been invited to sit in on this session.)

Others: Why are you here, Willy?

Do you know?
Willy: Because maybe the way I've been acting lately, very arrogant and not giving a shit about a lot of things I'm saying. Maybe this group can beat the shit out of me and blow my mind, and I can learn some things about listening to other people.
Others: What have you been running your mouth about?
Willy: Leaving.

Others: What's arrogant about wanting to leave?
Willy: I've been running my mouth about what I think about the staff, saying it's all fucked up, that there's favoritism.

(Pushed hard by the group, Willy owns up to being disturbed by a rumor that one of the staff is going with a girl in treatment.)

Others: But it's not true, is it?
Willy: No.
Others: But you were hearing the rumor for a week or ten days. Did you think of asking him? Look, if you want to find out something, you ask, unless you're looking for a way out, an excuse to split.

(Willy is really struggling with his uncertainties about the future, about leaving the house. After learning this, the group goes on to show him how he can start to demonstrate independence in other, less destructive ways.)

(Sarah is also preparing to leave the house. But she hasn't been able to find an outside job.)
Others: What do you want to do?
Sarah: I don't know.
Others: What can you do?

She wants to hang out at Phoenix.

You don't want to go to school, right? You want to go to work.

(Shouting) She's lazy . . . she's lazy . . . she's lazy.

(Sarah insists she has been trying to find work, but she hasn't been offered anything worthwhile.)

Others: You're too demanding.

> Look, I've got a couple of qualifications. But if I can't find a job I like, I take what I find. It's something. I can make some bread and look around for something else.
>
> You don't want to go to school. You're not qualified to do anything except waitress or wash dishes.
>
> *(Sarah has been looking for an office job. She admits she doesn't type too well, "But I took a test and, out of fifty people, I came in second." She has been offered typing jobs, but turned them down because they weren't interesting enough.)*

Others: You've been offered jobs?
Sarah: They were all typing, nothing else, no receptionist, just typing.

> *(The group now starts to shoot down Sarah's unrealistic goal, the supersecretary job she seems to want, because Sarah's real reason for turning down work is her fear of not making it as a typist. They try to boost her self-confidence, convince her that she really can do any of the jobs she's been offered, and that once she proves that to herself and her boss, she can work up to whatever she wants.)*

(Because of the group's experience, they were able to move quickly from subject to subject and get at real issues with a minimum of yelling, argument, or protest. Still, it took half an hour to get Mike open enough to start really looking at his attitude, while Sarah had to withstand a heavy barrage of indictment before she admitted her real fears.)

Most Phoenix residents are ready to move out, to graduate, after two years in the program. When they entered, they stopped using drugs and began to make real changes. Shy and defensive, ready to lie, refusing to squeal, they started to learn trust, honesty, and responsibility. They moved from fear and hatred of authority to acceptance and assumption of it.

And they come to enjoy Phoenix, for therapeutic communities are pleasant families in which to live. There is a rich emotional life and there are good times too: open houses, parties, sports. Many find leaving as difficult as arriving, and almost all keep in touch after they go.

Young residents often return home. If nothing much has changed there, they find the going rough, away from the community where they have been safe and supported in their new ways. Parents can prepare themselves for their youngster's homecoming by attending special encounters for parents. But the purpose of these groups is not merely to help families cope with their former drug user. They get down to root problems that endanger other, younger children, and parents can emerge from these groups with insights that strengthen their families and their marriages.

Part Two

To UNDERSTAND MORE about the ways families deal or fail to deal with drugs, a special series of encounters was held at Phoenix House during the fall and winter of 1970–71. Eight families took part. They were black and white, poor and nearly rich, single parents and couples. Phoenix staff members met with them, and the first six sessions were recorded. Notes were kept of later meetings.

From the transcripts and notes, as well as interviews with both parents and children, the following family portraits were compiled. They are not case histories, but records of how each of these families came to perceive, and how the group came to understand, the factors that hindered or prevented them from helping their children.

The three families have in common only the fact that they are intact and have each sent at least one child to Phoenix House. The portraits are not completely accurate; some details have been altered to allow the couples anonymity.

These are not average families, and yet they have common problems. Their problems prevented them from doing what was necessary or *all* that was necessary for their children, as your problems may stop you.

Not every parent who is immature, who drinks too much, or who works too much will have a drug-troubled child. Not every mother who seeks to dominate her mate will cause her daughter to act out. Ineffectual fathers or violent fathers may well have children who stay drug-free. But all such parents are handicapped. Should their youngsters go to drugs, they will need to deal with their own hang-ups before they can do much to help their children.

There is, in most homes, *some* circumstance that can prevent parents from doing what they must, should their children need help with drugs. These three families were trapped by such circumstances. Their problems are easy to see; the encounter drama makes them even more pronounced. But what is remarkable about these families is not their differences from other, more fortunate families, but their similarities. The differences are mainly a matter of degree, for most parents will be able to recognize some small part of themselves in one or more of these six men and women.

8. The Adamses

THEY'RE TOUGH, both of them. Life has never been easy for them, and they have never made it easy on each other. A chunky man, heavy shouldered and young looking, Bill, forty, is naturally soft-spoken. His wife, Carol, forty-two, dark and thin, seems brittle at first meeting, with plenty of surface toughness. They have been married for twenty years. Their son Eddy has been a Phoenix House resident for more than a year. The Adamses had been meeting with parents' groups even before their son came into the program.

(Bill and Carol were late for the first session. When it came their turn to tell something about themselves and Eddy, Bill spoke.)

Bill: Well, I have a son, and he says he started using drugs when he was fourteen. And I guess I knew it all along. I knew there was *something* happening. But it took four years for me to recognize the problem, four years and seven arrests . . . until he was where he couldn't get out of trouble, where I couldn't *not* face it. I mean, there he was — in jail. He had so many court cases that we didn't know one from the other. Then, I was forced to do something to help him. But for the first four years, I ran away from it. He'd say, "Well, Pop, I'll be good," and "It won't happen again." And, in my mind, I knew damn well that it *would* happen again. But I said to myself, "If

	I don't look at it, maybe it will go away." It never did. It just got worse.
Others:	Why did you do it?
	You must have given yourself *some* reason.
Bill:	No. I thought it was just a stage he was going through, that he was just taking a little, like the other kids do.

It was easy enough to see certain things if I'd wanted to see them. But I didn't want to see them. I wanted them to go away. I looked at some unbelievable things and didn't *see* them. One night, he almost burned the house down. And the next night, when I came in, he'd fallen asleep with a cigarette again. And I didn't bother to sit down and talk to him and find out what was wrong.

When a boy does this, he is reaching out for help. He is trying to tell you that there's trouble. But in our house, there was constant fighting, not just an occasional battle. It was constant, day after day, every day that we were together. We never had time to spend with the children. And I had my own problems within myself, and he had other problems, and this is how he showed us.

Eddy

The youngest of three children in the home, Eddy was the only child of Carol's marriage to Bill. He was a wanted baby. According to Carol, Eddy had had no difficulty learning to walk and he was able to read newspaper headlines at three. At five, he was dressing himself and became angry when his parents tried to help him. He decided what clothes he wanted to wear when he was eight and demanded the right to buy his own clothes at twelve. However, until he was eleven, Eddy continued to wet his bed. Neither Bill nor Carol paid much attention to this, assuming he would outgrow it.

In school, Eddy was a bright student and was kept in a class for intellectually gifted children from fifth grade through junior high school. But his schoolwork deteriorated in high school, when he was becoming seriously involved with drugs.

Life in the Adams home was chaotic through most of Eddy's childhood. The marriage was buckling under money pressures, for Carol admits to a hunger for better things than she has, better clothes, a better home. "It got so we couldn't stand each other," Bill confesses. He was periodically unfaithful; she drank heavily and began avoiding her home, hanging out in neighborhood bars.

Eddy remembers being "right in the middle of the fistfights when they happened, or the crying and the screaming . . . and all the things they said to each other." He also felt the competition for his love: "My mother would always ask, 'Who do you love more, me or Daddy?' And I always knew what she wanted to hear. She wanted me to love her more, and I felt I favored my father. I always loved them both, but I felt I favored him, and I felt very guilty about that." Still, he recalls, "When I was nine or ten, I honestly believed that if he got the hell out, maybe the family would straighten out."

Bill and Carol were then having troubles with the older children. "The older boy," says Bill, "he was the kind of kid who always made a lot of noise, a lot of trouble. What he was, was a pain in the ass. He'd wreck the house, fight, play with his sister, make noise. Eddy didn't do that. He was too nice all the time. He was always nice. Looking back, I can see that he was a manipulator. He got what he wanted by being nice."

Eddy began to go his own way. When he started with drugs, Bill and Carol were focusing their concern on their daughter, who was then acting out in other, more obvious ways. Eddy seemed to slide into the background, coming and going as he pleased.

It was Carol who first spotted something specifically wrong with their younger son — fresh needle marks on his arm. Bill couldn't be convinced that there was anything to become concerned about. Even after Eddy overdosed and the doctors showed Bill the boy's needle marks, Bill refused to face his son's druggism. Finally, when Eddy had been arrested a few times, Bill had no choice but to deal with what was happening. He and Carol went looking for help. They tried several addiction programs before coming to a Phoenix Center. None of the programs did much for Eddy, nor did the center — at first. However, Bill and Carol became part of a parents' group and began working on their problems. While Bill and Carol were emotionally involved in their son's drug use, there was little they could do to help him. They were dealing with him as dishonestly as he was dealing with them. Bill's refusal to recognize Eddy's druggism was his way of denying guilt for his part in it. Carol, who did recognize the problem, convinced herself that nothing could be done about it. "I expected him to die before he was twenty-four," she says. In fact, she hoped he would die. What she felt for Eddy was anger, not concern. This was her substitute for guilt and her way of handling her role in his drug troubles.

After Bill became aware of his own dishonesty, his own manipulation, he was able to do what was necessary to get his son into treatment. When Eddy was arrested for the seventh time, Bill resisted the impulse to head straight downtown and bail him out again. This time, Eddy stayed in jail until he was sent to Phoenix House by the court.

(During the second session, the group began to focus on Bill and Carol's dealings with each other. From what Bill had said at the opening meeting, it seemed that the result of their discord was a regular display of violence toward each other.

When Carol told how annoyed she was by a prolonged visit from Bill's parents, the group used this situation to move in on their real concern, how Bill and Carol meshed.)
Leader: How many times have you sat down together and

	talked about this and worked out ways of handling it?
Carol:	Him and I?
Leader:	*Him.* You keep saying *him.*
Carol:	Yeah. That's *him,* isn't it?
Leader:	I never refer to my wife as *her,* never.
Bill:	That seems to be the kind of relationship we have. After a year of encounters, we just haven't come to a common purpose.
Others:	(*To Carol*) What's your decision on his folks?
Carol:	Out.
Others:	Why?
Carol:	Because I want to be on my own. I don't want to baby-sit for two old people. I'm not ready for that.
Bill:	It's not because you want to be alone with me.
Carol:	That's part of it too. Yes, it is.
Bill:	You're talking about everything but the problem. And the fucking problem has always been you and me. It's always been you and me. You ran one way and I ran the other. (*He turns from Carol to the group.*) Does she want them out to be alone with me, really, or to go on about her usual life . . . to run out of the house, go to stores, keep running?
Carol:	You know, we can't get together on things. I don't know what to do.
Leader:	What about yourself? What do you want to change? Forget your mother-in-law.

(*Carol says that she would like to have an operation on her back, so she can go back to work. She talks about having more money. But the group asks, "Isn't there one thing about yourself you want to change?" They want to know why she has had trouble staying at home, why she must get out and away — but Carol sidesteps most of their questions.*)

Leader: Maybe I can come at it another way. You're like a dope fiend on the street that we get to stop shooting dope. You've given up some of your major symptoms. You've given up swinging nights, given up getting drunk, and I'm sure that some of the major battles that used to go on in the house are cooled because you've learned to use the encounter. So the encounter has cleaned up some of the gross symptoms. But you have to move beyond that. You have to move, and I think you are trying to avoid taking a harder look at yourself.

Others: That whole pattern of drinking and carrying on, how long did that go on?

Carol: A long time.

Leader: There are a lot of people who'd say, "Well, you've stopped the drinking now and live within the bounds of normality, and why don't we leave it alone." I wonder if you're satisfied with that.

Carol: No, I'm not. There's more. I know there's more. I just can't come out with it and say it. And I think this man and woman living in my home is stopping me from seeing it.

Leader: You know, it's always easier to relate to externals. It's always easier to relate to the mother-in-law in the house or your son who's messed up with drugs or your husband who's doing this or that. It's a good way of keeping from focusing on whatever it is about yourself.

Carol: But if I don't know, how can I tell you?

Leader: Well, why don't you try? Maybe you ought to know, at this time of your life, why you had to stay relatively drunk and on the loose for thirty years.

(Carol remains elusive. She talks readily about the things she wants — new cups and saucers, dresses,

blouses. "And I get pissed off when I haven't the money for them." But she resists any probing of her relationship with Bill.)

Others: At what point in your life did you feel . . . not at ease with yourself, that you didn't like yourself?

Carol: (*Flatly*) When I was sixteen and got pregnant. That's when the drinking first began.

(*Carol quit school then and married. But the marriage lasted only long enough for her to have her first child and conceive a second. When she was 22, Carol married Bill, bringing two children with her.*)

Others: You really have never grown up, have you?

You're really kind of a baby in a way, aren't you?

Carol: No, no. I'm not a baby.

Leader: Well, you want a lot of things. It doesn't sound like you want to give much . . . there's a lot of dissatisfaction with Bill. But you still can't have as much contempt for him as you have for yourself.

Others: What do you do, what do you do for Bill?

Carol: Everything that a wife does, and I didn't even used to do that much.

Others: Like what?

Carol: Cook, clean, and it's a lie when he says I don't screw. I mightn't as often as he wants, but I do do it . . . more often than I ever did.

Others: How often?

Carol: Once or twice a week. I'm still working in that area. There was one time, four years, I didn't sleep with him. He never touched me.

Bill: It's not going to change. We got together and decided that we were going to do something to help our son, and we're very respectable, and I come home from work every night. But we don't really do anything together. And I've sat down and told her how I feel, and she just doesn't understand. My idea is not being by myself, but being with my wife at home sometimes.

Like she doesn't really believe I can do anything. Her favorite expression is "you fucking jerk." She even says, "I love you, you fucking jerk." That's it in a nutshell. To her, I'm a "fucking jerk."

Others: How do you feel?

Bill: Like a fucking jerk . . . like I can't get it together in my own home.

Others: Why should you take it from her?

Bill: What should I do? Leave her? I don't want to leave her. I'll tell you what kind of a woman Carol is. She doesn't just have an argument. With her you have a knock-down, drag-out, fucking fight. And the police come, and it's a whole scene. I had twenty years of that shit. I don't want any more. And I don't want to leave her. I really don't.

Others: What holds you?

Leader: Before you answer that, do you think Carol has any idea about what it is you appreciate? I mean, you two seem able to shit on one another rather easily. Can you express anything else?

Bill: What it is I like about her?

Leader: Yes.

Bill: Well, she's clean.

Others: What else?

Bill: I like her. I've always liked her. I like the home she makes. I like the things she buys. I like her taste. I don't like her mouth, that's all. You can't have a discussion with her. It's got to be a big fight.

Others: What about sex?

Bill: Yeah . . . sex. See, now we can have sex any time we want to. The children are gone. Only she says no. She's not warm . . . very cold woman. I remember once in fifteen years . . . she put her hand on my head . . . and went like that (*showing how Carol had once stroked his head*).

See, then you turn to her and try to explain it, and she gets you in a fucking corner. I'm tired of telling her how I feel.

Leader: Well, maybe if you stopped using that language, maybe she'd stop too.

Bill: What language?

Leader: Fucking.

Bill: Aw, that's the way I am.

Others: Do you feel she has no respect for you because of your income?

Bill: Definitely. That's all I ever hear from her, how "I hate this house. I hate that. You don't make enough money. You didn't go to work today."

Others: I feel you don't respect yourself either.

Bill: No, I don't.

Others: So she doesn't respect you, and you don't respect you.

Bill: I married her with two kids, right? I used to work for the city, and I didn't mind working for the city. And then we had a baby, Eddy, and now I had three kids, and I made about sixty-five dollars a week. So I had to make more money, right? I waited tables nights. So I had two jobs, and I couldn't make it on two jobs. It was too much. So I went over to hauling garbage, not for the city, a private company. Now it was okay. As soon as I went on the garbage truck, at least we ate, we had some money. I wasn't happy, but I had a goal. I didn't go to school, I got no education.

Now, it's twenty years later. The kids are all on their way, and I hate this job. But I don't know what to do about it.

(*There is talk about other jobs for Bill, but he insists he can't make a change until Carol is willing to help him.* "I know I can make a living. I can get another job. And I know I can be happy with a lot of things. But I can't get together with her."

Carol, Bill insists, worries about where the next week's pay will come from. She claims to have gone along with him when he has tried to change jobs before. But it never worked out: "Because he's too slow with everything he does," *she says.*)

Leader: The image that keeps coming to my mind is this. We found you two in the ring with gloves on, and you were punching the hell out of each other's heads — constantly, day after day. Your children were looking around and running like hell away from it.

And now, we've given you a few tools, so that you can take off the gloves and sit down for a moment. But each time you hear a hostile word — you kind of jump up for the bell and start throwing punches.

Bill: That's true. We're ready all the time.

Leader: You're still a little punchy. You've been beating up on each other for so long, it's automatic. She sneezes and you say, "Gesundheit." You say, "I think I'll change my job." She says, "You're a fucking jerk." So you say, "Oh, you fucking bitch, you don't understand me." And that's the way it goes. You have a really infantile relationship.

Bill: How do we better it?

Leader: I think people here will give you a couple of ABCs. It's hard to write a prescription, or even put any Band-Aids on your cuts, when you don't even see there's still a problem, and that you have to make individual changes. You (*Carol*) sit back and point at him. He sits back and points at you. Nobody is saying, "You

	know what? I've still got to make some changes. I've got to do some growing up."
Others:	(*To Bill*) I wouldn't tolerate her crap for a minute, not for a minute, if I found myself that castrated. And I was at one time. I was newly married, and it took me six months to snap. I was doing everything right and everything was wrong. Because I wanted to please her so much, she'd taken my balls away.
	You've got to take some stands, whether she understands them or not. Go out there. She'll just have to live with some ambiguity while you're going through a job change.
	Only you're not going to change. You love it. You do.
Bill:	I don't love it.
Others:	You're so in love with it, man, you can't cut loose. You wouldn't let her go for any woman in the world. It's the safest thing you have. You're used to it.
	(*From a staff member*) I'm damned if I'd send your kid back to your house when he's ready, unless you make some real changes. I wouldn't send him unless he could come home to a human kind of environment and really see that his parents could live like mature adults, who care for one another and can be with one another and help one another and have a marriage instead of a slugging match.
	What is it about you, Carol, that keeps you locked in this bind?
Carol:	Well, I can't say it's comfortable.
Others:	You decided to stay with Bill. You didn't want to

	break up this marriage. So, why aren't you working, really working, to make it better? How do you feel when he says, "She could hardly put her hand on me and touch me?" He feels you think he's a "fucking jerk."
Carol:	No, I really don't. I think he's very smart. But he wastes his time, and he drags in all this other crap.
Leader:	It doesn't take much to ring that bell, and you're right in there accusing. I mean you can hear yourself doing that.
Carol:	Well, you know . . .
Leader:	Even if Bill made a resolve to really try and change some things now, you'd be ready, waiting for him to make the first little slip.
Carol:	No, no.
Leader:	It's got to be. It's automatic with you. You haven't taken a good look at how much anger you still hold for this man.
Carol:	(*Quietly*) Yeah, I hold a lot of anger.
Leader:	(*Very softly*) What're you going to do? I mean, are you going to continue, continue to keep dumping on him, keep pulling the rug out from under him? Because all you can do, all you can do now is perpetuate the situation you're in. You'll keep it going, keep nicking away at him so that he won't make a move.

(*Carol's façade is starting to crumble. She has been keeping the group at a distance, replying flatly, unemotionally to most of the questions. She has rarely looked at Bill, kept her eyes on the leader or the others. Now she leans forward in her chair, her eyes down, her voice heavy.*)

Carol:	I'm going to cry.
Leader:	Good.

Carol:	(*Sobbing quietly*) Because it's not what I want to do . . . not what I want to be . . . I try not to call him a fucking jerk. I can't find how to do it . . . he doesn't show me any way to stop it.
Leader:	(*Evenly*) You know, he may drop dead tomorrow, or go off a pier or something. You see, Carol, the problem you face is something that is very much a part of you. At this point, Bill just dances with you. He just reciprocates.
Others:	You know, Carol, I feel it isn't just Bill . . . you think all men are fucking jerks.
Carol:	That's right. I feel most of them are.
Others:	Because of what happened to you before you were married? Your other husband?
Leader:	Let's go back to you. Everybody wants to interpret for you. What were you feeling when you were talking?
Carol:	(*Slowly*) I was feeling that I really loved him, and I want to see him get ahead.
Leader:	How do you tell him that?
Carol:	I tell him.
Leader:	How?
Carol:	I kiss him . . . and in bed . . . maybe not often enough.
Leader:	I don't think you know how to say it. I don't think you know how to really get it out.
Carol:	I try . . . I try awful fucking hard. I really do.
Leader:	Why don't you look at him, at Bill?
Carol:	I'm like ashamed.
Leader:	Why don't you look at his face? Look at Bill and tell him what you think of him.
Carol:	(*It is hard for her to say this, and she is close to tears.*) I really love you . . . and I want to see you do better . . . and I never believed you loved me.

Bill: I didn't hang around for twenty years for kicks. I told you, time and again. It was you. It wasn't the kids. I didn't hang around because I like to support kiddies. That's what I've been trying to tell you for years and years.

(There's a rush of talk, a kind of backing away from the emotional impact of what Carol has said, talk about the difficulty of getting feelings into words.)

Bill: It's not *saying* "I love you." You do that often enough. It's the way you all of a sudden had to clear it up. You say, "I love you," and put your arms around me and kiss me and then you run somewhere else before we get anything together.

Carol: I really don't know what I'm running away from anymore. I just figure if I say I love you . . .

Bill: That will suffice, and you're off the hook.

Leader: You know, one way you can work with Bill and show him that you're willing to be close to him is to put aside some time you can spend with him . . .

Carol: In the bedroom?

Leader: It's got to be more than just the bedroom. If you just isolate it to an hour in the bedroom, then nothing is going to happen. Try to take on an attitude of wanting him and communicating.

(After some talk about Carol's boredom, the time she spends at Bingo, and Bill's reluctance to leave the house, the group moves on to the Adamses' earlier encounter experience, which one group member insists never got past "trading war stories.")

Leader: I'm sure everyone is tired of listening to you two going on: "Remember the time I whacked you up the side of the head . . . Remember the time the cops came and all the neighbors were upset."

Others: You go to encounters like other people go to church.
Bill: She has the idea that if we miss an encounter, Eddy will quit the program.
Leader: You know, your son's encounters and your encounters really don't have anything to do with each other. Maybe sometime in the future, in two or three years, when he's grown up and gotten something built into him that he can count on . . . maybe when you have gotten yourselves out of the ring and hung up the gloves . . . maybe you'll be able to have an adult relationship. None of that is possible right now. You two have a lot of work to do. You really have to start where you are tonight and work hard at building something happy. It isn't enough to have stopped cracking each other over the head.
Others: What are you feeling, Bill?
Bill: I know I'm a lot to blame. Lots of times she turns me down and I get mad. But I don't want to lose her.
Others: How'd you feel when Carol said that she loved you?
Bill: I don't quite believe it.
Others: You're a son of a bitch.
Leader: You're doing the same thing that she does. You just told her how lousy you feel when she says, "You fucking jerk," right? So she opens herself up and is straight with you — and everybody here is very touched by Carol's openness. It is a beautiful thing to see. And you sit there . . . "Oh, I don't really . . ."
Bill: I'm not that trusting where she's concerned.
Leader: But, you see, Bill, it's the same thing. The first little thing that doesn't sound right and Carol will retreat. Instead of being open with you, you'll be a "fucking jerk." And yet you can't keep this thing open and let it grow. You're much more comfortable being in the untrusting position, in the distancing position,

	in the putting-her-down position. I mean, you keep up with Carol. That's what I meant before. I think you're both punchy.
	I don't know your son. I know where he is, but I don't know him. I do know that all of this, all you've been through tonight, all the problems about trusting and being close and tender, all the problems about being able to love, they've got to be his problems too.
Bill:	You mean, because he never saw anything else.
Others:	That's the model he learned.
Bill:	But he knows we've changed. He always says, "Boy, there's some changes here," when he comes home.
Leader:	Because there have been changes. I'm sure he remembers lying awake, time after time, afraid that you were going to literally kill one another. So, it's a great relief for him to come in and find relative peacefulness.
	You see, kids get terrified of their own rage. Little kids feel rage, and it scares hell out of them. It may be rage at not getting a bottle or rage at their brother or rage at you. They feel it, and it frightens them. But if you demonstrate that you can control these same feelings, it comforts them. When they see *your* rages, then they're not sure they will be able to control what goes on inside them.
Others:	And kids know. We all think we can close the bedroom door and the vibrations won't go through. But they do. They all go through.
Leader:	Can I put you both through what may seem to be a minor motion? Could you spend the next week, until we get back together, not mouthing a single profanity at one another? Not one obscenity?
Bill:	I'll try it.
Leader:	Nothing. No bitches, no bastards, nothing.
Carol:	That's not so easy.

Leader: I'm aware of that. I'm hoping that little symbolic effort may jar you enough to remind you to be careful. You need to spend a lot of time being careful with one another's feelings, trying to be sensitive to each other. You've been lashing out in such an infantile way that you've lost any softness.

(At the fourth meeting, the group initially focused on another couple, whose problems are somewhat similar to the Adamses'.)

Bill: (*Making a point about scrambled communications*) Last night, I wanted to tell Carol that I wanted to stay home alone with her. What do you say? It was so fucking hard . . . it didn't come out right . . . I said, "You know what I'd like to do? I'd like for you and I to stay home and watch television." She said, "You fuck, you want to do that again."

It was so hard for me to put it right to her, that I just wanted her to be home alone with me. I thought it would be nice.

(*After continuing with the other couple, the group gets back to Bill and Carol.*)

Others: (*To Carol*) Weren't you on a profanity bond?
Carol: Yeah, and I'm still using it.
Others: Your old man asked you to stay home and share his genitals with him . . . your response to this was, "Oh, fuck."
Carol: It . . . it's hard . . . I look around the house and I see there's no more kids there. I only have him. And he says, "That's all there's going to be from now on."

We were so alone the other night. Suddenly, it was just him and me . . . and I was scared.

I get pains in my ears, pains I never had before . . . changes.

Bill: When she went through this nonsense, I used to say,

"Ah, screw you. I don't need it. It's never going to work out." But, last night, I stuck to my guns. I told her, "You know, it's you and me." I told her some of the things I felt, how I wanted to be alone with her. And she went through all these changes and pains and heart attacks.

Leader: (*To Carol*) When Bill says he wants you to stay, what goes through your head?

Carol: If I stay, what's going to happen? What are we going to do? What *can* we do? There isn't anything to do in the house. So, I start running and cleaning . . . mirrors that don't need cleaning.

Leader: It's amazing, isn't it, that people have fantasies about being shipwrecked, with nothing to do except hang out with each other and share one another's company. You finally get all the stragglers off your island and want to run out to Bingo.

Others: When you think of being alone with Bill, what do you think about?

Carol: That it's boring. Let me *do* something. I can't just concentrate on him.

Others: When you *are* alone with him, what do you feel?

Carol: I always feel like . . . let's blow this place, let's go where there's lots of people.

Others: Carol, obviously you're going to be alone together, and there's going to be more opportunity for sex play, right?

Carol: But we did that the other night.

Others: Listen to that: "We did that the night before," with a kind of distaste.

Carol: It wasn't distasteful.

Leader: I believe it wasn't distasteful. Yet, something seems to happen to you after that experience so that you start to close yourself off, become unavailable. You

	get pains, you run to doctors. The ability to be open is foreign to you.
Carol:	No, it's not foreign to me.
Bill:	Like, each time I would have to go through a whole number . . . through another three weeks . . . before I could get to her.
Others:	When you've had sex together, do you feel good about it afterward?
Carol:	Yes, I do. I feel good about it.
Others:	Please don't try to sell that to us if it isn't that way.
Bill:	No, it's not that way. Let me tell you what she does after it. She finds an excuse to start fighting.
Carol:	Well after it, I say, "Let's go somewhere and *do* something," . . . and he don't want to go. So then I say to myself, "I'm sorry we did it."
Bill:	See, it's like I got to pay a price. She sets a price on it.
Others:	All he wants you for is your body?
Carol:	Yeah.
Others:	Like he abused you, and now he's ready to dump you?
Carol:	I get that feeling. But I do enjoy it, but only for a few minutes. It doesn't last.
Others:	It's when he's directly on your clitoris and you're getting direct pleasure. Then it's okay. But the minute that stops, you start to close up and feel uncomfortable about having been vulnerable.
Carol:	Does that mean I don't like sex?
Leader:	It doesn't mean you don't like sex. It means that it's very hard for you to maintain a feeling of being open and receptive and ready. And you have to recognize it for that and not go back to thinking, like a high school girl, "You just want me for my body, you just want to use me."

Carol: Yeah, I feel that.

Bill: It's always like she did something for me and didn't get anything out of it. It's like last night. We had sex in the afternoon. I would have to go through a whole number to get her involved again. And she knew that, and that's when the pains started.

Leader: (*To Carol*) Emotionally, you're kind of a virginal high school girl. You may have been around, but you've never gotten beyond the point of grabbing a little quickie. You're very close, and it's hard for you to stay open. And you'll save yourself a lot of money and grief if you'll stay out of doctors' offices, running around and having them check out your heart. When that happens, and you put your guard down and your Bingo card down and lie down . . .

Bill: Why is that so hard? While it's coming on, she loves it.

Leader: As long as she doesn't have to do it mentally. As long as it is a direct, physical act, then it's easy.

(*To Carol*) Remember, the last time we were talking, we talked about the same thing, only we were talking about it *above the belt,* about letting yourself be open and not slugging back.

Carol: The minute it's over my mind is on something else. And when that's over we've got to do something else, until we go to sleep exhausted.

Leader: And in that way, you are never in a position of being open, of saying, "Bill, I want you. I want you to stay next to me. I want you to be close to me and love me."

Carol: Because I never said it to anybody like that.

Leader: But if you said it, you wouldn't be running all the time and cursing all the time.

Others: And beginning to *say* those things, you may begin to feel them.

Leader:	Remember what Bill said to you a little while ago. He said he would like you to stay with him. A very simple thing, very basic. "I'd like you to stay with me. Please stay with me."
Bill:	See how hard it was? I couldn't just say it that way last night. So I said, "Wouldn't it be nice if you and I go home and watch TV?"
Carol:	But it didn't sound interesting to me.
Leader:	What about the coded form in which it came? It was rather indirect. And you didn't listen to what the real message was. It was all together with the television, but he was saying he wanted to be with *you*.

(Bill and Carol, whose encounter experience was richer than those of other couples in the group, eventually made some sizable changes. They were forced to look at the ways in which they rejected each other and refused to accept warmth and tenderness from each other. It wasn't necessary that they recognize and understand everything that affected their behavior. They only needed to uncover enough to get a handle on their problems and turn them around.)

9. The Browns

THEY ARE VERY QUIET. A small, reedy man with thick gray hair, David slouches and hunches to make himself even smaller. He is forty-six, but seems older. Ellen, forty-three, a neat and competent office manager and housewife, has resigned comfortably into matter-of-fact middle age. The Browns have been married for what might have been nineteen uneventful years, were it not for their one child, Jill, fifteen, a Phoenix resident for almost one year.

(David and Ellen were among the first couples to arrive at the group's initial session. Their turn came early in the meeting, and David started off.)

David: Well, my name is David Brown, and the first thing that happened to us was when our daughter was involved in an overdose of pills. We got her to a doctor right away and tried to find out why she was taking these pills. And I thought that if I frightened her that she wouldn't go into anything else.
Others: How old is your daughter now?
David: Fifteen. She started at fourteen.
Ellen: We had a lot of trouble with Jill . . . the way she was fooling us, the way she was fooling the psychiatrist. He finally got disgusted himself. He was the one who told us about Phoenix House.

She didn't want to go to school. She played hooky. And she was taking drugs . . . She was coming in at

	three, four o'clock in the morning. We were walking the streets looking for her. That was the worst year of my life. We never knew if she was alive or dead or where, so we kept looking and walking.
Others:	In other words . . .
Ellen:	For one year, she was on drugs.
Others:	Do you know what she thought she was doing?
Ellen:	You couldn't really get into a conversation with her . . . because she was an addict . . . You just couldn't. Maybe now she could carry on a conversation. But before, I think she felt that the world was against her. She just kept running.
Others:	How did you find out?
Ellen:	About the heroin? I never knew . . . and she would take it in the house. She had friends staying with her, and one of her friends told me. I didn't believe it. But then I realized it was true. There were some things missing from around the house. She stole some money from me. She sold my husband's camera. A little watch, she sold. Little by little, things were missing. Then, I think . . . she wasn't selling . . .
David:	They were using her like a delivery girl.

Jill

A good baby, her mother remembers, she ran almost as soon as she could walk. As Ellen tells it, Jill was a loud, bustling tomboy who enjoyed games, other children, and animals. Jill remembers differently. She was a lonely child, who had pets (dogs, rabbits, mice, even snakes) but no friends and was always fighting with other children.

From nursery school through sixth grade, Jill was sent to private school. She did well there but felt that she was "missing something" by not attending public school and finally convinced her parents to let her attend the public junior high. David and Ellen were reluctant to make the change and regretted it almost at once. Jill became a discipline problem in her new school, talking in class, wandering about the room, ignoring her homework. She still showed potential and was quick to learn, but she was easily discouraged and apt to lose interest. Her record was dismal and she was constantly in trouble. At home, she set her own hours, ignored bedtime. "All she wanted to do was watch television," Ellen recalls. Jill wanted things her own way and got them.

Ellen and David did not realize that Jill had started raiding their liquor cabinet. She would become sickly drunk whenever they were away but was careful to add enough water to the bottles she'd tapped so that her parents never became suspicious. However, she wasn't able to keep her glue sniffing a secret. She began coming home late at night, became sloppy and careless. Her clothes were often marked with traces of glue. When confronted by her mother, Jill admitted sniffing and promised not to do it again. But nothing Ellen or David were able to do, or were willing to do, was strong enough to counter their daughter's druggism at this point.

The friends Jill found were older than she. Sometimes she brought them home, but usually she went out at night to meet them. Often Ellen and David would go looking for her in a park near their home. One night they found her lying on the ground, unconscious from an overdose of barbiturates. Although she again promised her parents that she would stop using drugs, Jill soon moved up to heroin.

Once they knew their daughter was heavily into drugs, the Browns did act quickly. Jill was seen by a psychiatrist, sent to a detoxification clinic (where she stayed for only a few days), and taken to a Phoenix Center. She refused to attend the center, however, and her parents took her to juvenile court.

The court sent Jill to Youth House for three weeks. Then, she was given a choice of returning to Youth House or going to Phoenix House.

Although the Browns appear to have a stable, even a static

marriage, there were some obvious frictions in their home. David ran through a series of low-level jobs before Jill was in junior high school. He now works for the state. A conscientious parent, David spent a lot of time with his daughter, taking her to parks and zoos, to basketball games and the beach. Yet he feels Jill was ashamed of him. She would become embarrassed when he showed affection in public or joked or sang or danced. Usually a timid man, David hit Jill once, when he found her drunk in the park; another time, he tore an earring from her ear, causing some bleeding. He still feels guilty about those things.

Ellen has other regrets. Although Jill confided in her, Ellen was quick to believe what others said about her daughter. She feels she should have shared more with Jill, but she is not exactly sure what she should have shared. Ice skating is the only example she offers. While the times he struck his daughter seem to weigh on David's mind, it was actually Ellen who most often punished the girl.

The Browns had met with parents' groups but were not yet comfortable in the encounter situation. They did recognize that Jill had been totally spoiled, that she had realized little pleasure from the many things she was given, and that she was almost completely out of control by the time she moved into a therapeutic community.

(At the group's second meeting, the Browns were seriously encountered for the first time. Earlier in that session, the group had focused on Bill and Carol.)

Others: *(To Ellen)* How did you feel when you heard Carol talking?
Ellen: I felt that I shared a few things with her.
Others: Tell us about them.
Ellen: David didn't make enough money, and I had to go to work . . . which I still do. I'll always have to work to have the things I want. And, in the beginning, I

	minded that, but now I really don't. When I stay home, I get bored and go crazy and I feel I have to go out.
Others:	Tell us a little about you.
Ellen:	Things are coming up now . . . since my daughter got into trouble . . . things that I never realized. I must have been doing wrong . . . I don't know . . . I thought I had a nice life. I could find some things wrong with it, but I was very happy with my husband. We didn't fight so much. We get along nicely. We go out together. We like the same things. We try to be nice to each other.
Others:	What do you want to change?

(Ellen knows that she appears to be — indeed, she is — the dominant spouse. She is quick to admit to her bossiness and tell how she is trying to change it. "I always knew I was stronger," she says. "Now I'm trying to push that strength on him." In spite of her good intentions — "I let David talk now, let him try to do things for himself" — she complains he is "slow . . . he doesn't open his mouth" and still depends upon her. "Like shopping for clothes. He doesn't like to go without me. And I don't feel it's right. I feel there are certain things he should be able to deal with himself.")

| Leader: | Why don't you tell us what you feel. How do you feel about Dave? |
| Ellen: | I love him . . . and if there's anything I could do for him, I would do it . . . and I feel that he has a lot to give that he doesn't give, that he doesn't have enough feeling for himself . . . He doesn't get the right words out. He doesn't have confidence in himself for anything. Like, he's in a civil service job. |

	But he won't take the test to move ahead. "Oh, I won't pass," he says. And I try to tell him to go to school and to *try,* because I feel that even if you don't pass, you've got to try. But he feels he can't. And I get very angry at this. I feel people can get ahead if they only make up their minds to it.
Others:	Do you think he should be as aggressive as you?
	Do you think that under this . . . this passive man that maybe there's a real man?
Ellen:	(*Rattled*) He's not mean.
Others:	Do you think that under this backwardness . . .
Ellen:	I think that when he was a young boy his sisters tried . . . tried to make him feel that *this* was him, and that's all there was to him. In other words, they never gave him any encouragement.

(*David has said nothing through all of this. He watches Ellen with vague approval, as though she were talking about someone else.*)

Others:	So you're the boss, right? You're the big boss?
Ellen:	Because he's pushed his business on me all my life, all the time we're married. If I say, "What are you going to do?" he says, "Whatever you want." If I say, "What would you like, red or yellow?" he'll say, "Yeah."

(*There is a long hassle about who pays the bills. Ellen tries to explain why she feels she must do them and what happened when she tried to give the job to David.*)

Ellen: Because I gave him the checkbook . . . and I gave him all the bills, and I walked away one time, and he says, "What are you doing to me? I can't do it."

	He gave me the bills to pay when we first got married. He said, "You're the business woman. You pay the bills." He still says it now.
Leader:	So what has really changed? I mean, maybe you're a little more subtle in handling the situation. You might not talk about it as much, and you might not push him as much. But I don't think that really shows there's been change.
Ellen:	Well, I think he's changed a lot.
Leader:	In what way?
Ellen:	He's more outgoing.
	(*No one believes this.*)
Others:	How did you feel listening to Ellen running her story, talking about your sisters and what you do and don't do with the books?
David:	(*Softly*) I felt a little ashamed.
Leader:	That's it? Just a little ashamed?
David:	(*Even lower*) Maybe a little weak . . .
Leader:	You don't feel angry?
David:	No.
Leader:	Never feel angry?
David:	Oh, I feel angry from time to time. But not like this. Because I thought this was . . . I thought you were trying to help me. I don't think anybody's here to harm me. So why should I be angry if somebody's trying to help me?
Others:	What makes you angry?
David:	Anybody that tries to push me around, tries to take advantage of me.
Others:	Your wife too?
	Do you think Ellen has ever tried to take advantage of you?
David:	No. She's tried to help me. She's out for my welfare

	... And I feel that she loves me ... and that our marriage isn't all push from one side. I feel that we try together on things, try to work things out.
Others:	It doesn't sound like you try to get together. It sounds like you try to accommodate yourself to what Ellen wants.
David:	Maybe I *was* like that. It's a short time since this thing came about. It'll take me a little while to step up to changing myself.
Others:	You couldn't take over the books?
David:	Well, she said ... she's good with figures. I'm very poor at them ... Because I'm not much ... I didn't get much of a real education. I stayed back. I was in an accident where I had five years of trouble ... and ...
Others:	It's easy for you. She's the big business woman. But what about the other things? Can't you decide between red and yellow? Can't you buy your own suits?
David:	Well, I pick out my suits. I decide the store. I'm just asking for a second opinion.
Leader:	How do you understand what happened to your daughter?
David:	Well, I think that she thought maybe I was ... I wasn't there enough. But I think, when the chips were down, I always came across ... And I think I was a good person, getting along by myself. I made up my own mind what I wanted to do. Whatever I do ... I do pretty good.
Others:	What do you do for a living?
David:	I work for the Department of Motor Vehicles ... a clerk. And I think I'm one of the best clerks in the department. I think I do a very good job.
Others:	You never want to go further than that? You're content?
David:	I'm not content with it ... but I do a good job. I

don't think I'm a coward, and I don't think I'm a sissy. I think I'm as much man as anybody . . .

Leader: When you say that you don't feel like a coward, you don't feel like a sissy . . . I don't get the feeling that you really believe it.

David: (*Shakily*) Well, that's your opinion.

Leader: Yes.

David: I mean, you're entitled to your opinion, right? I know myself better than you do . . . I mean, I don't think a man is a man just because he can go in a bar and hold three or four drinks.

Leader: I'm not talking about realities. I'm only saying what I *felt* when you said, "I don't feel like a coward," and, "When the chips are down I always come through."

David: When I had to put my daughter into Youth House, I did what I had to do . . . as a man.

Leader: Do you realize that, even as you're talking, you seem to be almost whining? You present yourself apologetically.

David: Well, I realize that I have faults.

Leader: I'm not trying to knock you down.

David: You're trying to help me.

(*Through all of this, David has hunched down in his chair, rubbing his hands together, sometimes hugging himself or covering part of his face with his hands.*)

Leader: I asked you a question about your daughter, and before you finished with it you apologized about a dozen times. Dave, what did happen with your daughter and Youth House?

David: Well, I made every step that was necessary. I went to . . . I took her to court, and I said, "Look, I want my daughter put into this Youth House . . . because I have to help my daughter." I said, "I want my daughter in this place . . . until she's ready to go

	into the Phoenix program. I committed her. I told them she was shooting dope.
Leader:	So when the chips *were* down, you did come through. Can you tell us more about your daughter?
David:	Well, as I said, I thought I was a good father and showed love.
Leader:	When you look back now, how do you put the pieces together?

(The question was asked of David, but Ellen interrupts, drawing the group away from the notion that David's weakness might have been cause for Jill's acting out.)

Ellen:	I suppose we gave her too much. I worked and he worked. She went to a private school. Anything she asked for, we went out and got her.
Others:	You were trying to buy her love.
Ellen:	No. I just felt if she wanted something she should have it.
Others:	Actually, you did it because you knew she didn't have any real home life.
Ellen:	She had a home life . . . I only worked part-time until she was about eleven or twelve. If she came home at five, I was home at five. If she came home at three, I was home at three.
Leader:	You were telling a story, Dave. What happened to it?
David:	Well, I still feel I did everything any father would do for a child . . . love . . . took her places . . .
Leader:	How did you handle it when she got mad?
David:	I would tell her off. You know . . . I'd yell at her.
Leader:	It's very hard for me to see you getting angry, laying down the law.
David:	Well, I'm not steady. I mean I might go one week, and then the next week I'd let things slide, because I don't like to argue too much . . . That maybe was

the wrong thing . . . I'm still trying to be more of a man . . . more aggressive.

(*With David stuck firmly on how he is trying to improve, the group turns to Ellen.*)

Others: Jill must have known what you felt, that you wanted your husband to be more successful.

Ellen: Well, she might have felt that maybe her father didn't make enough money, because her mother had to go to work.

Leader: You're getting subtle about it. I'm sure that Jill heard you bitch at Dave because he wasn't making enough money.

Ellen: I didn't bitch that much. I knew I *had* to go out to work.

Leader: Look at the way you express yourself here. People pick it up right away, how you take over . . . and put him down.

Ellen: (*Honestly distressed that it shows*) Do I really put him down?

Leader: Yes, you really do. Now, that's not very difficult. He makes it easy for you. He bends over and practically starts to crawl. Dave won't even stand up straight. He holds himself in a very frightened posture.

Ellen: When I met Dave he stood that way, and I used to say, "Can't you straighten up?" And his daughter said to him, "My friends laugh at you because you look like a hunchback." It didn't make any impression on him. All he said was, "Your friends aren't so pretty either."

(*David wins some approving laughter for this one.*)

Others: Your daughter felt that your wife was always the dominant one, the person who made decisions. How do you think she felt about that?

(David falters, starts to answer, but stops when Ellen replies, denying what the group now recognizes as the basis of Jill's drug use.)

Ellen: She played one against the other. I don't make *all* the decisions.

Others: But she was embarrassed by the way he looked. She was talking about his not being decisive, being wishy-washy.

(To David) How do you feel about everybody sitting around saying how fucked up you are?

Aren't you mad at us?

David: Give me a reason why I should be mad at you.

Bill: Well, I think you're a fucking jerk, just like Carol thinks I am. I think you're a Caspar Milquetoast, who can't make a decision.

Others: Everyone views you the same way.

Leader: Amazing, isn't it? You're sitting here with a bunch of brand-new people, and they all snap that feedback at you. They're very consistent. They don't believe you. They think you've lost touch with your feelings, that you're kind of turned off.

David: Okay, suppose that's true. What's the next step . . . for me to change?

Leader: We know something now about the way your daughter felt. We know that you didn't ring true for her, that she couldn't look to you for a certain kind of standard that she wanted.

David: *(Impatiently)* Okay, so what's the next step? For me to change?

Leader: Dave, you're all hung up on changing. You don't see that there are some things that come first. You can't even see that there's a problem. You're so embalmed in your own fluid.

You remember when we were talking about Bill and Carol being kind of punchy from what they've been doing? Well, for the last forty-some years, you've been walking around like Caspar Milquetoast. You've just . . . lost touch with yourself. I don't think that you're lying to us, in the sense that you're trying to be tricky or manipulative or insincere. I think you don't hear anymore. Like a guy who's been working with a jackhammer and can't hear fine noises anymore.

You've become such an accommodating person . . . you're an appendage. You are so willing to go along that you don't even feel anymore what most people feel in their bellies when something jars them. You can get right next to somebody, and he can really be grating on your nerves, and you don't even feel it. Those nerve endings have become very insensitive, and it's going to take some very hard work for you to open those endings up again and get to feel things. You're a very turned-off guy.

Others: Are you afraid?
David: Who's afraid?
Others: You are. You're afraid to say anything that might antagonize anyone.

You probably can't.

Bill: If I call you a fucking jerk . . .
David: I'll say you're crazy.
Bill: Well, you are a fucking jerk.
David: (*Tentatively*) And you're crazy.
Others: When you say that, though, it doesn't sound real.

He's not real. Don't believe him.

Why don't you tell them the truth? You're not such a goody-goody as you're making out to be.

	Come on, tell the truth.
David:	Where am I lying?
Others:	Tell them how you can lose your temper beautifully.
David:	Well, I can lose my temper.
Others:	Tell us about it.
David:	This one time with Jill, I knocked her to the ground. And there was another time . . . I slapped her so much that she started bleeding at the ear. And it was too much . . . I'm a different person when I lose myself. I lose too much, and I was afraid of hurting somebody.
Others:	That's the only time?
David:	Well, there was one time . . . I was on the street and somebody said something to me. So I said, "Why don't you mind your goddamn business?" But when I do lose my temper, I get too carried away, and I get upset . . . upset stomach and everything else. But if you push me a little too much, I'll push you right back . . . I won't take it.
Leader:	I don't believe you.
David:	Well . . . try it.
Leader:	See, what you did with your daughter was comparatively safe. You made some remarkable retort to a passing stranger, who you'll never see again, never have to confront again. That isn't the same thing as sounding off to someone who'll be able to get back at you.
David:	I'm not afraid to tell you off if you said something wrong.
Others:	What can we say that would be wrong . . . that you're disgusting . . . that you're a disgrace . . . that you're a rotten father? You're a nebbish.

(With insults and goading, the group tries to draw some kind of angry reaction from David.)

Others: David, I feel so bad for you.
David: Why?
Others: Because you aren't fighting back. I feel terrible. I can relate to you in a way. But I'm trying to fight back. You just sit there and take all this shit from everybody.
David: What do you want me to do?
Others: *Say something.* Show your anger.
Bill: Do you think your wife's ashamed of you now?
David: She might be a little bit.
Others: She's beyond it already. She's seen you take so much of this she could tolerate anything.
David: No, she couldn't.
Others: She does, she does it well. She's a professional tolerator.

Everyone here thinks you're an asshole, and everyone here isn't crazy. Everyone here . . . I'll personalize that . . . I have no respect for you, and I'm not crazy.

David: Well, before this time is over, you're going to change your mind.
Others: Why should I change my mind?
David: Because . . . when the time comes . . . I'll learn enough to be able to tell you what I think of you.
Leader: Would you like to be able to do it now?
David: In time, I'll be able to tell them off.
Others: He asked you if you would *like* to do it now. We recognize that you *can't* do it now. But would you like to? Would you like to be able to do it to anyone?
Leader: Maybe you don't feel like telling us off. Maybe you feel like something else.
David: I still think you're trying to . . . do good.
Leader: Forget that. What do you *feel*?

David: Well, I still feel nervous (*pauses and turns to the leader*). Okay, does that satisfy you?
Leader: I can believe you.
Others: Yeah, that's reasonable.
Leader: Tell us a little more about that. Where do you feel nervous? In here (*rubbing his hand across his stomach*)?
David: No. Up here (*touching his throat*). You know, I shake when I talk, and it's a hard thing to get over. What's the use of kidding myself? I've been this way for a long time. Somewhere along the line I went wrong . . . when I was a kid. (*He starts to retreat from the present, from what he is feeling.*) When I had this accident . . . and I had thyroid trouble. Maybe my father was so thin cut, and I sort of followed in his footsteps. I mean, I'm still trying to find out where I went wrong.
Leader: Tell me more about that nervous feeling.
David: Well, I'm starting to get over it.
Leader: No, no, no. You're giving us all that history. I'm talking about here and now. You said you felt nervous.
David: Well, now I'm starting to loosen up . . .
Others: He asked you . . .
David: (*Shouting*) I'm talking to him. You mind your . . . business.

(*This answer, the first honestly angry response from David, brings shouts, cheers, and applause from the group.*)

Leader: Where do you feel nervous?
David: Well, like sweaty hands.
Leader: Right. What else?
David: That's all. I felt that . . . I thought that . . . as I go along I get less nervous.

Bill: You said one thing tonight, Dave, that everyone thought . . . was an honest statement, was credible. You said, "I felt . . . I feel nervous. I'm kind of new at this." Now when Mitch tries to pursue this feeling, you keep justifying it, explaining it. Everyone feels nervous. Everyone in this room feels nervous.

(*Others join in, trying to get David to talk about his feelings, but he falls back to his old line.*)

David: I think you're just trying to bait me to get angry.

Leader: Nobody cares if you get angry. Nobody cares if you get happy. Nobody cares whatever you get. What we want is for you to talk about being angry or happy or nervous. Your problem is that you come out with that same old garbled line of bullshit regardless of what you are feeling. You come out with that same note, and it makes you a very dreary fellow.

David: I'm not trying to be dreary.

Others: Yes, you are.

You're a product, Dave, of forty-six years of acting a certain way. You're just like Bill, who was so in love with a situation that was so messed up. You do your best to be dreary. You practice it all the time. You work on it with fervor.

Dave, you won't even admit to being messed up.

David: I did admit it.

Others: Now you do. But it took more than an hour and a half for you to admit you were nervous.

David: I thought it was obvious.

Others: You were sitting there saying, "I'm not a coward. I have courage," and it was all a lot of shit.

(*This line continues for a while, with little reaction from David, until Carol joins in.*)

Leader:	The only person here who seems able to push your button a little bit is Carol.
David:	Because she's afraid of people, afraid of psychiatrists.
Carol:	And who are you afraid of?
David:	Nobody.
Carol:	Liar.
David:	You're still afraid of men. You said so about three dozen times in the meeting. You're just covering up . . . covering up for yourself.
Leader:	Dave, you know you're talking about *yourself*, don't you?
David:	No, I'm not.
Leader:	Afraid . . . afraid of men . . . afraid of psychiatrists.
David:	I'll tell you again, I'm not afraid of anybody.

(By the end of the second session, the basis of Jill's druggism was apparent. A dominant mother and an ineffectual father will often have a drug-troubled child. Children are confused by the reversal of roles; they regard with contempt a weak father who is bullied by his wife and resent a mother who tries to replace him. Jill, who identified with her mother, took on many of Ellen's hostile ways. This showed up early in her aggressive behavior with other children, the reason she was lonely and friendless.

Since Ellen was unable to run the family by herself, there was a kind of power vacuum in the home. Jill desperately needed to be brought under control. She kept probing and poking past the boundaries of responsible behavior, leaving all kinds of clues to her indiscretions and attempting to discover some limits to what she could get away with. She never found them. There was no point at which her behavior brought a consistent and convincing "no" from her parents.

Only when David and Ellen learned that Jill was using heroin did they act forcefully enough, using the courts as leverage to pressure their balky daughter into treatment. They were helped by the psychiatrist and center staff members who supported their decision to use the courts. If they had been able to act with that much certainty earlier, when Jill was signaling frantically for help, they might have been able to stop her druggism early on.

The Browns were not the hardest-working members of the group. In later sessions, David was able to talk more freely and take part in more of the encounter, but he made only small changes. Still, he believes that he has come a long way. This belief has made him somewhat more secure about himself, his job, and his dealings with Ellen.)

10. The Cowans

THEY ARE WARY, but less of others than each other. Frank, robust and fifty, is a hard-selling businessman. Gayle, a handsome, frightened woman, still hasn't decided which side of forty to try for. They have been married twenty-two years and have four children: Steve, nineteen, a Phoenix resident; Sylvia, a troubled thirteen-year-old; and eight-year-old twins, Sharon and Sean. The Cowans have been to parents' meetings, have had some experience with encounters, but know much less about themselves than they realize.

(Frank, a naturally aggressive type, led off the first meeting.)

Frank: My name is Frank Cowan . . . Before I found my son in the hospital, my wife told me that he was on drugs, that he had stuff in his room, and I failed to go along with my wife.

My son was an honor student, and all of a sudden his marks dropped. They want from ninety to seventy, sixty, fifty, and my wife felt that he should go to a psychiatrist. So we sent him to a psychiatrist for two years. He was going to the psychiatrist and fooling him. He was telling the psychiatrist what he wanted to hear, and he was taking trips. He was coming home at eleven or eleven-thirty after taking his trips at five or six o'clock.

One night my wife and I came home just before one in the morning, and all the lights were on and my older daughter ran out and told us that the police were taking him out in an ambulance from an "overdose" of LSD, speed, and a bottle of wine. He also drank half a bottle of whiskey . . . all in one night. He took marijuana . . . everything. He was out to destroy himself. And when I got to the hospital he was in pretty bad shape. And then I realized he was conning me, conning the psychiatrist.

Others: How old was your son when this happened?
Frank: He was eighteen.
Others: When did he start taking drugs?
Gayle: About fifteen, when my mother-in-law was sick, and Steve was stealing some of her Demerol. He was drinking cough medicine too. Then one day he had this new friend. And I asked a neighbor about him and she told me the boy went around selling drugs. And as soon as I was off the phone, I went to Steve's room and looked in his drawers and found a bag of marijuana. I told the psychiatrist, and he told me to get off his back and leave him alone, that Steve was just experimenting. But I wanted him to have a urine analysis. Frank said it wasn't necessary . . . and it came back all right. But I still didn't believe Steve, and I kept searching his drawers. I never found anything . . . and then after that bad trip with LSD I took him to a center. And after a while he said, "Mother, I think I'm ready to go to Phoenix House."

Steve

The oldest of the four Cowan children, Steve remembers the days before Frank made big money, when they lived in a small West Side apartment, before the larger apartment in Riverdale and the big house in Queens. Frank had to borrow money from his family when Steve was born, and he kept borrowing during the boy's early years. Arguments about money were constant, and Steve heard many of them, even saw his father beating his mother.

He was his mother's boy all of his childhood. Frank was rarely around. When Sylvia was born and Gayle became busy with her new baby, Steve became quiet and withdrawn at home. Still, he was active in school, a good student who was kept in accelerated classes through junior high school. In high school, he went out for sports, swimming and track, and placed high in city-wide competition.

Steve saw more of his father as he grew older. Frank took him to hockey and basketball games. "He attempted to have fun with me," Steve recalls. He supplied the boy with a hefty allowance, plenty of clothes, even ten dollars a week for a hair stylist. "But we rarely sat down and talked about our differences or our feelings."

About the time that his school marks began to drop, Steve started coming home late at night, dragging in tired with puffy eyes. His parents sent him to a psychiatrist. To raise his grades, Frank hired a tutor. But neither the grades nor the boy changed much. While his mother suspected his involvement with drugs, nothing was done until after he had a very bad trip. Steve had been into one drug or another since he was fifteen, although he never hit heroin.

Sylvia

The Cowans' older daughter, thirteen, talks constantly about running away and, more recently, about following her brother into Phoenix House. She is a lonely child, without many friends. As she displaced Steve as Mother's baby, so the twins have displaced her, and she envies the attention her older brother's drug problems have earned him.

(At the third meeting, the group first dealt with another couple whose problems included a history of violence and then turned to the Cowans. Frank had already admitted his "hostility." In fact, he seemed almost proud of his "tough guy" record.)

Others: What about you, Frank, how does this bounce off you . . . all this violence . . . and the kids?

Frank: Well, I'm a very hostile person. I used to hit my wife. But I work on it. I started working on it at an encounter.

Others: How about your kids? How do they handle the violence in your house?

(*Frank says that there is not much violence his children see.*)

Frank: Most of the time I'm home, I'm asleep.

Others: Why?

Frank: (*Blustering*) I work seven days a week. I'm forced to, because of my business. You want a little background on me? About ten years ago, I didn't have six dollars and seventy-five cents to pay a phone bill, and I owed about twenty-five thousand dollars. Today, I make fifty thousand a year, and I don't owe anybody a dime.

Others: All this security, how secure does it make your children?

Frank: Well, securitywise, I'm certain they feel . . .

Others: They feel the rent will be paid, there'll be food on the table and clothes for them to wear. But how about other security? Living in a home with parents. Have you provided that?

Frank: Not completely, no.

Others: You've got a daughter, thirteen . . . From what I hear, she can't stand being home. She wants to live at Phoenix House. She can't stand the constant fighting . . . She feels she's living on the edge of a vol-

	cano. I can understand her wanting to move into a house. She sees something that would be safer.
Frank:	I understand.
Leader:	I think you're letting yourself off the hook when you talk about how you're working on your "hostility."
Frank:	I have a lot of pressure on me. But I'm trying . . . it's hard for me . . . the type occupation I have . . . I'm worked up. I have to be on the ball. Because if you're not on the ball you don't survive. And when I get home, it's difficult for me. I bring that hostility home . . . It's hard for me to pull the switch.
Others:	What's your business?
Frank:	I own a liquor store uptown . . . and it's rough up there.
Others:	I don't understand why you have to work seven days a week.

(*This starts Frank off on how complicated his business is and why he can't leave the paperwork to someone else. He insists that he tries to make it up to his family by taking them on vacations and out to dinner.*)

Frank: But there are things about my business that nobody else can do, things I don't want to divulge to anyone.

(*Frank has it all worked out. He is hostile because he is pressured. He's pressured because he works too hard. He works too hard because his business demands it. The trouble is the business, not Frank, and the group must get past all the business troubles to reach him.*)

Others: What about bringing work home at night?
Frank: I do.

Others: Then you can leave your store early?

Frank: I can't leave early, because when I leave my men are afraid. I don't want them to quit, because I have very competent men. But they're afraid . . . and I'm not afraid. When I'm there everything works.

Others: Then hire a guard.

What would it cost you?

(*Frank carries a gun and has used it to stop robberies. He argues that a guard would discourage customers. Others reply that a concealed gun doesn't discourage many robbers.*)

Others: You don't have to take that risk. You can hire someone for that. Only, you kind of like the idea. How long have you carried a gun?

Frank: More than twenty years.

Gayle: (*Shrilly*) Twenty years ago, you didn't need a gun. But you loved having a gun. You loved the idea of being a policeman. You liked that. You said so. Even when you went on vacation, you always told someone you had a gun . . . And you still always show your gun. You either take your jacket off or let people know you have it. You'll meet a total stranger, and you'll tell him that you carry a gun.

And you don't trust anybody. No one. You could leave early at night. But you're afraid to leave the keys. (*She becomes more excited as she goes on.*) And you repeat and repeat and repeat . . . always asking me, "Is it okay . . . is it all right . . . is it okay . . . all right?" And I'm beginning to get sick over it . . . And any time I want money . . .

Frank: What are you talking about?

Gayle: What did you say to me about money a few weeks ago? "This is *my* money. My blood money. I worked for it. It's mine. And *I'll* tell you what to do with the money. I'll always keep the money 'cause I'm the boss. I've worked for it . . ." And all these years we're married, whenever I ask for a raise, money for the house, you pick a fight with me . . . I always have to account to you if I spend anything extra. You were always tight with money.

Others: Do you realize that the best thing that ever happened to your kid was that he shot dope?
Frank: He didn't shoot dope . . . close to it.
Others: Whatever he took. It was the best thing that ever happened to him. Otherwise, he might never have gotten out of this. *You* won't get out of it. She won't let you out. You won't let her out.

(Gayle starts on Frank about their daughter, who she claims is afraid of him, but they slide into an argument about their anniversary, which he passed up to play poker.)

Leader: *(To Frank)* How do you feel about the fact that your daughter wants to come here? You're a successful businessman, making fifty thousand dollars a year, respected and kind of feared in the neighborhood . . . and your kid wants to move out of your house.
Gayle: She hates living with us.
Others: What about the fact that your daughter is scared to talk to you or even scared to talk to your wife because she might mention something to you?
Frank: She calls me, she speaks to me.
Gayle: Not about what bothers her, not about sex. If I wear anything short or tight, she screams and starts to call me names. And she says, "Sex is *dirty* and I don't want to talk about it, Mother. If I do, you'll go back and tell Daddy."
Leader: Frank, all you talk about is the way you've improved,

	the vacations you take your family on, the dinners you have with your wife . . . You won't do any self-scrutiny . . . What about *you,* Frank? Can you hold a mirror to yourself and talk a little bit about the things you're doing week in and week out that are screwing up your house, screwing up your wife, screwing up your kids?
Frank:	I'd tell you that the big problem is my hostility.
Leader:	How does that come out? How do you show hostility to your wife, to your daughter?
Frank:	When I come home . . . the few times I do come home . . . my wife will be yelling at my daughter . . . but really *yelling.* Now, I have it rough where I work. I like peace and quiet when I come home. *Please don't yell.* Yelling presses my button. If she could only speak to me calmly, then it would help me to feel calm.
Others:	You say you only come home occasionally. . . . When *do* you come home? What *are* your hours?
	(Frank goes through a prolonged grilling on his weekly schedule. With the store, his accountant, dealers, his poker game, and what he does for Phoenix, he's rarely home before midnight.)
Others:	When do you have time to be so hostile?
	When was the last time you sat down and talked to your daughter?
Frank:	About two weeks ago.
Others:	What did you talk about?
Frank:	We talked about smoking.
Others:	When was the last time you sat down to talk with the girl with no particular problem . . . just to talk?
Frank:	I tried to talk to her about sex . . . and she just got up and went out of the room.

Leader: Frank, you can't talk to her *now* about *anything*. You can't artificially say, "It's Sunday morning, time for me to talk to Sylvia," and then go plop yourself down and announce: "Well, Sylvia, come here. Father is here. And now we'll talk. Let's talk about smoking . . . or let's talk about sex . . . or let's talk about something else." Because all you are doing is getting something off for yourself, assuaging your own guilts. And you can't artificially impose that on a child. Conversations between parents and children kind of evolve out of a relationship. You've got to be around and available . . . and listening, so that you can pick out the special times that kids are asking questions . . . and they'll ask them if you're listening.

Frank: Sylvia asks me questions every day. She calls me up for that.

Others: She's not telling you about any of the things that concern her personally.

Frank: No, she doesn't.

Leader: And she's not going to. You see, Frank, you've really gotten yourself to where you're breathing and feeling and wallowing around in your success . . . but you're an absent parent.

Frank: (*Embarrassed*) Most of the time.

Leader: You can't influence your daughter's life by plugging in for an occasional hour. It won't work that way. You have to bag a lot of apples with no specific motive. You've got to be there, and by your presence you say something . . . about yourself, about the way you handle things, the way you handle your woman, the way you're available and receptive. And out of that will come questions.

(*The group is now fairly certain that Frank main-*

tains his elaborate work schedule because he really doesn't want to be at home.)

Others: Is being home distasteful to you?
Frank: Not at all.
Others: Is money more important than your kids?
Frank: *(He hesitates)* You're asking a very hard question.
Others: It *must* be difficult.

Why did you have children? You don't really care for them.

Frank: I certainly care for them. I want to help my children . . . I'm building a future . . .
Others: Do you really think money is going to buy happiness for your children?

You lost one already.

Leader: Why don't you want to be home? I think everyone here is convinced that you work very hard — not to be home.
Others: You're full of shit. Now, you may have some good reasons why you don't want to be home. You may have come to some compromise you don't even want to talk about. That's your privilege. But don't try to pass that business shit off on us.

What are you getting outside, you're not getting at home?

Frank: On the rare times when I do come home, my wife is very unpleasant.
Others: Never go home . . . never talk about your wife. Do you like her?
Frank: Yes, I love her dearly.
Leader: If you love her, why don't you do something to cultivate the relationship? What you're doing now is kind of dying alive along with your kids. How long

The Cowans

before the twins start freaking out? And you're finding a lot of reasons not to go home and see this weird relationship. You find it more pleasant to fool around the store.

Frank: You don't understand anything about my business.
Others: Do you *like* your wife?

Do you feel friendly toward her?

Do you kiss her when you come home at night?

Frank: Yes.
Gayle: No, you don't. You think I'm a schmuck.
Others: Frank, is she your friend?
Frank: She's my friend. Without question, yes.
Others: How involved is she in your business?

How much does she know about your business?

Frank: Not a damn thing.
Others: Why?
Frank: Because my business is my business. I don't trust anybody. And every time there's an argument . . . she says, "I'm leaving." The first things she says is "I'm leaving." So, I can't trust her with money.
Leader: I'm sure you haven't even begun to run down your beefs at Gayle . . . You're holding all the good cards for later. And the reason is that you don't really want to change what you are doing. You're really very satisfied. You love running around with a swagger and a gun . . . the whole bundle you carry around. And you don't really want to change that. The fact that your marriage is going down, that your kids are going off . . . you really couldn't care less. Frank wants his cap gun and his boots . . . Frank wants his toys . . . his playthings . . . his malted.
Others: You know, you're a kid . . . tremendously self-indul-

gent. You don't think about other people, not about your wife, not about your kids. Not really. You pay lip service . . . "Yeah, I love my wife." But what the fuck do you do for her? Loving means *doing* something for people . . . giving . . . being sensitive. Do you think because you give her an allowance, throw her a couple of bucks, that you're showing love? What do you *do* for her?

(When the third session ended, the group had a good idea about life at the Cowans'. Frank isn't there most of the time, Gayle feels inadequate, and each is quick to abuse the other. Although Frank no longer knocks Gayle around, he did when Steve was younger. As a result the boy felt both angry and unprotected. Frank's rampant materialism and grandiose ways made him unable to share any feelings with his son, to admit to any uncertainties or weakness. In order to compete with his father, to be a man like Frank, Steve thought it necessary to be as big and as strong and as unreal. He played the "hero," the "big man" with drugs.

Sylvia is troubled by her burgeoning sexuality, which she tries to deny by denying all sexuality, particularly her mother's. This is not uncommon, and most secure parents are able to help their youngsters work out this conflict. Gayle, however, is thrown by it. It serves only to heighten her insecurity.

As the fourth session began, Gayle announced that she wanted to divorce Frank. Frank's response was that he too was ready to split.)

Gayle: I want to leave my husband . . . I feel we haven't really changed anything within ourselves. I still feel his anger, his hostility . . . so much that I get all closed up when I'm with him . . . and someday there'll be an eruption. And my daughter wants to go to Phoenix House.

Frank: That's a lot of blarney. You want to listen to a thirteen-year-old child? Tell them what happened since the last encounter.

(And Frank and Gayle are off and running down a list of grievances, starting with a fight in a restaurant soon after they left the last meeting.
The group squelches the haggling, then questions Gayle about her plans for divorce, which turn out to be vague and unconvincing.)

Frank: Excuse me, Mitch, may I say one thing, please? I was in a shoot-up this week.

(Frank's store was held up by two men. Frank shot one. His story, offered as a reason why he might have been difficult during the week, wins him no sympathy from the group.)

Others: You've been hoping this would happen for years.

You carry a gun so that you can shoot somebody, don't you?

(Frank insists on replaying the hold-up, defending the use and possession of his gun.)

Leader: I'm trying to tell you that I recognize, and I think a lot of people here recognize, that carrying a gun is all tied up with your sense of security, your sense of feeling strong and capable. If you were to shelve that gun, you would go through a whole series of experiences . . . like anybody kicking a habit.

(Frank agrees to try leaving his gun at the store.)

Leader: By itself, this isn't going to change your personality. It may give you some signals, and if you listen to them and use them honestly, they may put you in a position to make some changes.

	I have another suggestion for both of you . . . and that is to suspend any decision about getting separated or divorced. You know your marriage has been rocky for a long time. It didn't get rocky during the last four weeks. And what's happening is that we're stirring up a lot of shit. Because if there's a chance of salvaging the marriage, it's in dredging some of this stuff up and dealing with it and coming to some new realizations about yourselves.
	But each time there's an argument . . . each time we dredge something up, you threaten to run off, Gayle, or Frank threatens to run off. You keep that kind of game going and you can't ever profit from anything that goes on here or work anything through. So, I'd like to see a moratorium on divorce threats.
Frank:	I only said that once. She's the one that says it.
Leader:	The first words out of your mouth tonight were, "I'm splitting."
Frank:	I'm only flesh and blood, and I work very hard. And when I come home I want to come home to . . .

(*The previous week had not gone well for the Cowans. They match charges of coldness and hostility.*)

Others:	Frank, are you afraid to show your affection?
	You *are* afraid to show affection . . . to show weakness . . . to show your vulnerability. You equate being affectionate with being soft, being tender, being a sissy.
Frank:	There's something to that.
Others:	When your wife calls you a son of a bitch, do you feel more hurt or more justified? More right? Like you're doing the right thing by putting her down. If she lets you have it, then that makes you feel more right about not being home all the time.

Frank, what do you respect about your wife?
Frank: She's very clean ... an immaculate woman. She's a good woman. And she's not a run-around. She's very respectable.
Others: Could you tell Gayle some of that directly?
Frank: (*To Gayle*) You're a very respectable woman. You're very clean.
Leader: I'm sure there are *other* things you want to say.
Frank: I enjoy having sex with her.
Others: Is she an honest woman?
Frank: That's one thing ... She is honest ... and she's got a big mouth.
Leader: How about talking about Gayle to Gayle? You're talking about "she."
Frank: Do you want me to say only good things? (*To Gayle*) I had a lot of respect for you, Gayle. When I lost money, you weren't lazy ... You pitched in and tried to help get me out. When I ask you, you do some of the books, which I appreciate. When my mother comes you're nice, and that gives me a good feeling.
Others: That was nice.
It didn't hurt, did it?
Leader: How do you feel about that, Gayle? Can you tell Frank about it?
Gayle: You always call me stupid, and it's true that I'm a sponge. If I make a mistake, I'm afraid to let you know it ... 'cause I know you'd knock me down about it. I can't speak to people ... and you always say I'm stupid and I always feel unhappy.
Frank: I don't think I've done that bad.
Others: Gayle, are there things about Frank that you like ... that you want to tell him?
Gayle: Well, he is ambitious ... He always tried to get

	ahead . . . and better our family . . . Frank, I feel that you have a drive in you . . . that you drive yourself to where you can't relax . . . that you *have* to work . . . and you don't want to stop.
Frank:	Don't I try to change pace and take you on vacation?
Gayle:	Every time we go on vacation, you are always saying you're doing it because of me. If you'd say you're doing it because of me *and you* it would make me feel much better.
Others:	How about his personal qualities? He talked about yours . . . that you are responsible . . . respectable.
Gayle:	Well, I always felt you were a flirt. I always felt that was important to you . . . that women look at you . . . and you flirted with them.
Others:	You know, there are probably some things about Frank that you really appreciate but just take for granted.
Gayle:	Well, you care about the family, you do care about the kids.
Frank:	What would you like me to do?
Gayle:	Come in smiling . . . forget about the store.

(*This leads them back to the usual argument about who walks in at what time and with how much hostility.*)

Gayle:	I'm filled with guilt . . . I feel very inadequate . . . I always feel I'm not good enough. Just like two years ago, when I got my driver's license . . . and he had promised me the car once a week. But I never got it because he said he didn't give me a test of his own. So, I haven't driven since . . . Now when I think of driving, it frightens me.
Others:	Don't you feel you are trapping her? She already passed her driver's test. Aren't you putting a trap up

	for her when you say she hasn't passed *your* driver's test?
Frank:	Do you want me to tell you how she drives?
Leader:	Let's go back to something you said earlier, Gayle. You said you wanted Frank to be less hostile. Can you put that positively?
Gayle:	Yes, if he came in and smiled and came home and said hello, it would give me a good feeling.
Leader:	You don't want much. You can get that from the Fuller Brush man.
Gayle:	Getting it from my husband is much different.
Leader:	Is that all you want? We're playing Santa Claus tonight.
Gayle:	That isn't the only thing . . . He's a penny pincher.
Others:	Well, what else do you want?
Gayle:	His anger . . . his money . . . his repeating.
Leader:	What do you *want*? You keep telling us these negatives. You keep pressing those buttons, "He's a penny pincher . . . he's always repeating . . . bzzzz . . . bzzzz . . . bzzzz." How about something you *do* want?
Gayle:	A man who is friendly . . . who doesn't question something if I buy it on my own . . . a man who will let me feel free, instead of dominating me . . .
Others:	There you go again . . . Bzzz.
Leader:	You've got a wide-open opportunity here . . . a group that is ready to support your every infantile wish . . . and you can't even articulate one. Let's take a little trip. Let's say you're not married to Frank . . . You're not talking about Frank. You're talking about the ideal man . . . Now, what do you want?
Gayle:	First, he would be friendly . . . and he would think about what I said to him . . . would have considera-

	tion for my thoughts and my feelings. He would ask me, "How was *your* day?" We would do things together. And he would respect me.
Leader:	It doesn't sound to me as though you are asking for more than good manners.
Gayle:	I want him to . . . like me.
Others:	Do you know what you *avoid* talking about?
Gayle:	Love?
Others:	Yes.
Gayle:	I was thinking about it the other day. Maybe we are both . . . maybe I'm so immature . . . that I'm so selfish with what I want . . . maybe I can't love.
Others:	I don't get that.
Gayle:	Maybe I am thinking so much of my own wants . . . my own needs . . . that I'm not giving any love.
Others:	Well, are you?
Gayle:	I don't know. We fight most of the time.
Leader:	You spoke about all these things . . . affection . . . politeness. But what does Frank want? What is he missing?
Gayle:	*A woman.* I don't think he thinks of me as a woman. I feel he dominates me and orders me around like a child.

(*The group takes Frank and Gayle through some reruns of their late-night show, when he comes home.*)

Leader: Gayle, we suggested that Frank do something about himself. I would suggest that you stay up and cook him a few meals . . . in the most kindly way possible . . . even if it's twelve at night.

What we're asking is that you put yourselves through some changes that no one expects to be easy and painless. Because you're so insecure in your relationship that you don't want to change anything.

Why don't you guys court each other a little bit? I

can't get over how dead you are . . . how turned off you are. And you break out of this trap like the Frankenstein monster . . . with abuse toward one another. There is no softness, no easiness. He maintains his distance and you maintain your bitter whining.

But your answer to this is to announce you're going to split. Rather than face yourself and take some difficult steps to break out of that prison you've built for yourself . . . you would rather jump out of the whole thing. Of course, it wouldn't make any difference. You'd either be alone and bitter or find another guy and replace the whole situation in six weeks.

Gayle: I was thinking about that . . .

Leader: Basically, your wants are so small. You're asking for some good manners. That's all. You are not asking for warm and open gestures. You're not asking him to come at you with love and affection. Nothing like that. You are asking him to respond, to say hello.

Gayle: I feel it's a beginning . . . That's something.

Leader: You've been starving, right? And you're asking for a slice of bread and butter. You're not asking for a meal. But I hope you will set the table.

(The Cowans arrived separately for the fifth meeting. Gayle waited until Frank was on hand before she started.)

Gayle: I've been trying to have a better relation with our daughter, Sylvia, but I find that all my inadequacies are preventing me . . . and I'm struggling . . . and I can't stand the struggle much longer. I cry a great deal and I'm depressed. But I understand what's wrong with me, and I don't know what to do about it.

I play the role of mother to my husband . . . and my daughter is always talking about going to Phoenix.

When I get up, she tells me she thinks about what she's going to take with her when she goes.
Yesterday, we had an accident . . .

(And Gayle is into a tale of Frank's latest clash with Sylvia, manhandling her in a restaurant. Frank starts to explain that it began when "She called me a name.")

Gayle: You know, Frank, *you* yell, you get kind of fresh.
Frank: She abuses me . . . She called me a dirty name and I won't tolerate that.
Gayle: You've called me a few . . .
Frank: Would you take that from your child, Mitch?
Leader: Yes, within boundaries and limits. The point is that where does she ever get the chance to tell you what she thinks or feels?

(Frank moves off the subject of Sylvia and tells about his last meeting with Steve, who was back from Phoenix House for a visit, how he told the boy his plans for bringing him into the business.)

Frank: I explained to him that I wouldn't be doing him a favor, that he'd be doing me a favor. I said, "I'm going to make money on you." I related to him, and he said he felt very good about that.
Others: But Frank, if he wants to live on his own . . .
Frank: I said, if he could do it financially . . .
Gayle: You said, "You *can't*, Steve, because I have to support you while you go to school."
Frank: Well, I feel a boy who goes to college . . . I thought I would help him. I am financially able to help him . . . I would gladly help him.
Leader: His concern, at this point, isn't your financial ability to help him. It's his ability to become a man in his

own right . . . how he could earn that without having to depend on your favor and your goodness, which might be very good in its way, but might not make him feel like his own man. When you can listen more, you'll begin to hear other meanings in what kids are saying . . . and hear things on a couple of levels.

As conversations like that get richer, and you exchange more, they keep rounding out. And you know what? They can start out on a very ugly note. They can start with a fight.

Frank: I feel that I have advanced a certain amount. Like Steve said the next time he gets out, he might not want to spend time with me. I said I understood, because he wants to take out girls too. I said, "If you get permission for the car . . . I will give you the car."

Others: There you go.

Frank: You mean that was the wrong thing?

Others: He's obviously striving to get some feeling of his own worth . . . But you want to make it easy for him. How old is he now? Nineteen. Does this kid feel right about driving a great big Jaguar? No way in the world.

Frank: Should I give it to him, if he gets permission?

Leader: It's not the specific, not offering him the car. It's the principle of *listening*. He wasn't asking to borrow the car. He was only asking you for one kind of permission. "Can I have a little more distance? You know, it's been nice to talk to you, but if I didn't want to come next week, would you mind?"

Frank: I told him I didn't mind.

Leader: *That's all.* That's all he was asking.

Others: Frank, you were saying the same thing with Gayle. You want to give gifts at times . . . and lay things on people . . . and that's your need more than theirs.

Leader: Does it make you feel good to see him in the Jag? You know whose cars kids generally smash up?
Frank: Their fathers'?
Leader: Did you ever dig why that is? Why kids smash them up? The father is generous, he puts all this on them, he says, "Here, son, take the car," and the kid promptly goes out and destroys it.

You see, on some levels kids know when they are ready to handle things and when they are not. When you lay something on them that they can't handle, they become angry at you. And angry kids will punish themselves by getting into accidents.

(*Gayle forces the talk back to their daughter, Sylvia, whose friends are smoking marijuana.*)

Others: I think you ought to tell the children's parents.
Gayle: Sylvia has to face these children in school.
Others: So what?
Frank: She said that if Gayle ever did that, they'll never talk to her. They will call her a rat. She won't have any friends at all.
Gayle: These are friends that she grew up with . . . and now they're smoking pot instead of taking pills, and I should tell their parents. And she is very vehement against it.
Others: Do you want to tell them?
Gayle: Yes.
Others: Well, why do you feel so terrible about it?
Gayle: Because she gets so angry about my mentioning it.
Leader: That kind of blackmail goes on all the time, right? Your daughter has to be home at ten-thirty or eleven. She says, "All my friends are coming in at eleven-

thirty or twelve, and if I have to come home at eleven, I'm breaking up the party . . . They're not going to talk to me. All my friends are going to think that my parents are rats."

Have you ever eavesdropped on a private conversation where your kids told about coming home a little early or something else that you demanded of them? What they say is, "I guess my parents are really concerned." That's the message that comes across. So, what are you going to do? Are you going to give her permission to carry on some kind of mock popularity contest?

Gayle: No.

(The Cowans are off and running early in the sixth session reporting their latest contretemps, the most recent fight. Although much of the week had passed quietly, the level of anger was up to normal in time for the meeting.)

Leader: Frank, are you telling me that Gayle didn't make some attempts?
Frank: She did.
Others: Significant attempts?
Frank: I would say so.
Leader: That's very obvious. It's obvious to everyone here.
Frank: Yeah, but you see . . . any little word I say . . . I feel like I'm walking on glass, and any minute the glass will crack.
Others: Right. But doesn't that go both ways? It really sounds like you were kind of laying for her.

How did you feel that Gayle was willing to accept some of the information she got here last week?

Frank: I felt good about it.
Leader: Frank, every week you come in here with a charming vignette from the week before. And every one of

these things is a document. Every week you've got to document how right you are . . . and how wrong your wife is. And this week you almost didn't make it. You got all the way through the week before she finally came through for you.

(Frank goes into his hostility bit. "That's my main problem. I'm hostile." But the group isn't buying it. "Half the guys in the country come home beat, wound up, or tense.")

Leader: If you can share a little bit of yourself, Frank, that's a very important thing. It makes you more whole. It'll touch Gayle in ways she can understand, and she'll relate to you in a more human way. Right now, you're asking her to tiptoe around and serve you dinner . . . and make believe. It's not real at all. Everything real gets tamped down . . . it keeps getting tamped down. Only, these things blow up.

Others: I'll bet Frank never came home and said, "You know what, Gayle? I'm fucked up and tired."

Did you ever feel like dumping the business?

Frank: Sometimes.

Others: Do you like it? Do you like your business?

(And that starts Frank onto how important his business is, how hard it is, and how hard it is for him to unwind.)

Others: You don't try to unwind. You have very little ego strength . . . discipline. The minute anyone says anything . . . you're off. You have no tolerance for pain at all. You're like a kid.

Frank: I couldn't be successful if I was like that.

Others: How the hell do you figure you're successful?

	He makes money.
	We're not talking dollars and cents.
Frank:	In the business world, everything is judged by money.
Others:	Sure, but Gayle isn't in the business world. Your son doesn't live in the business world, and neither do your other children . . . so, neither do you.
	It's very convenient for you to maintain this notion that all you have to relate to is the business world. Of course there are no feelings involved in the business world. You never have to be open about your feelings or yourself. You make your profit and you take it . . . you don't have to *feel* anything.
Leader:	Let me stop you here. I want to hear from Gayle about Sylvia.
Gayle:	She still wants to go to Phoenix House . . . She's very upset and angry . . . and yesterday she spoke . . . she was very cruel to me the night before.
	(*Sylvia had fought with her mother when Gayle told the other parents that their girls were smoking marijuana. Gayle had asked Sylvia to bring this up at Phoenix when she visited there on Saturday afternoon.*)
Others:	What happened . . . that was Saturday night?
	How was she cruel?
Gayle:	She said, "Drop dead . . . You're a witch . . . You're a bitch . . . I hate you."
Others:	What did you do?
Gayle:	I told her to go to her room.
Others:	How did it get kicked off?
Gayle:	I asked her if she had asked them at Phoenix about

	what I'd told her . . . about telling the other parents . . . and she started to get very angry. What am I going to do with her? I'm scared.
Others:	And that's all? Is there any more to it?
Gayle:	I spoke to her about whatever she's taking. I felt she was taking something. Even though she told me she only tried pot twice, I feel she's lying. She told me last week she tried meth, and then told me she was only saying it because she wants to get into Phoenix. So, I don't know what to do or whether to believe her or not.
Leader:	Look what you did. You sent her to Phoenix and, in effect, what you said was, "Take up what I told you there and see if Phoenix doesn't agree. Because you really won't accept what I say . . . since I don't really feel like I'm boss. Phoenix will have to do that instead of me. Let Mother Phoenix tell you."

Then she comes home, apparently loosened up and tenderized . . . maybe she heard a few dirty words in the encounter . . . and she decided to tell you what she felt. And she got up all this stuff. And what did you do? You told her, "I don't want you to talk that way to me. What you have to say is cruel. It is, in fact, forbidden, because when you talk that way to me I will put you in your room."

Remember last week we talked to Frank about letting a situation happen where a kid could say all that . . . where he could call you a son of a bitch. |
| Gayle: | She's doing it . . . and I resent it . . . I wasn't able to be effective speaking to her . . . I didn't know what I had to do. |
| Others: | That's just the point. Because you don't feel effective, because you don't feel that ultimately you're the boss . . . because you feel that Phoenix is the boss instead |

of you, you end up playing tit for tat with her. "Well, you say that, then I'm going to put you in your room." Why couldn't she tell you these things? Why couldn't she call you a witch or a bitch? That's what she felt.

Gayle: But I thought a child shouldn't behave that way.

Others: She wasn't behaving in any way. She wasn't out in public shooting her mouth off. She wasn't shooting drugs. She wasn't breaking up the furniture. She wasn't *doing* anything. She was just talking, and she was telling you how she felt. Now if you summed all that up, what she was in fact saying was . . . that she was scared she was going to lose her friends. That this meant a lot to her.

So why couldn't you have heard all that vomit come up and realize that what she was afraid of was losing her friends? And then tell her that you understand how she feels . . . but that doesn't mean you're not going to call her friends' mothers. Tell her, "I think that's wrong, and I'm not going to allow you to smoke pot either."

Gayle: During the week, I tried to call. I had to go outside, because she kept taking the phone out of my hand. She wouldn't obey my orders: "Get away from me, let me make the call."

Others: But you told her before you were going to make those phone calls. It never occurred to me that you would make them in front of your daughter.

Gayle: (*Flustered*) Even after I talked with her, I got angry because I know . . . I understand that she is frightened, I understand how she feels.

Leader: You don't understand. If you understood you would let her sound off . . . and not be threatened by it.

	Why can't she do in her home what you do in your home? You get pissed off . . . It's "Fuck you, Frank" and "Fuck you, Gayle."
Gayle:	In other words, you sanction a child . . .
Leader:	I sanction your setting limits by the way you act yourselves. You think that kid is going to buy the bullshit that she can't do what you do? Never in a million years. Nor should she. You have no right to set limits on her that you won't live with yourself. You don't have that right.
Gayle:	Well, my feelings were that a child shouldn't behave this way.
Leader:	And my feelings are that adults shouldn't behave this way either. Sure, you wouldn't want her shooting her mouth off like that four times a day. But, she has a lot of feelings and you've got to let her blow them. That doesn't mean she can do what she wants. It doesn't mean you will let her get away with lying. It doesn't mean that you will let her get away with staying out late and not obeying rules. There's a great deal of difference between what she does and the kinds of things she says. You know, we try to put kids through some artificial molds, into little cookie patterns that make no sense for them at all. In fact, it just enrages them. They know how angry they are. They know they would like to turn around and hit you . . . or yell at you . . . or something. And you say, "No, no, we don't do that." Of course, she hears you in the bedroom, dining room, basement, and Jaguar: "You fuck . . . you this . . . you that."

You know, even if you two were under much more control, so that you weren't carrying on at home, even then your kid might have the need to dump some feelings. |

Gayle: I didn't realize . . . From the way I was brought up . . . a child just doesn't talk that way.
Others: The way you were brought up has made you into a loud, foul-mouthed bitch. So, it didn't really work terribly well, did it?

(*The group pulls Gayle back to the phone calls.*)
Gayle: My daughter says that once I tell their parents . . . the children won't socialize with her anymore. She went to school with the kids since elementary school, and they're all the same age . . . They're the only girl friends she knows.
Others: Unless she's going to smoke pot with them, those friendships weren't going to last a hell of a lot longer anyway, were they?

She may have decided she was going to go along. That's another decision she may have to make or has already made . . . It has very little to do with your phone call . . . but a lot to do with you.

Gayle: She said that she wouldn't do it anymore.
Others: But what about those other kids?
Gayle: I spoke to two parents . . . One told me, "My daughter says it isn't true." I said, "Well, I know you're not going to believe me because I'm a stranger . . ."
Others: You don't think they're going to be watching their daughters now?
Leader: Gayle, what will happen to Sylvia if she doesn't see these friends anymore?
Gayle: She will have to make new friends . . . She'll just have to.
Leader: What I want to know is why she can put you over a barrel so easily.
Gayle: Because I'm unsure of myself.

Leader: Are you afraid of losing her friendship?
Gayle: Yes, I am. She's constantly picking on me . . . She doesn't like my wearing contacts . . .
Others: She doesn't like you wearing contacts . . . She doesn't like your looking sexy . . . doesn't like your husband to touch you. She doesn't like a lot of things, and she lets you know it. In all of these things, she really muddles you up. You get all confused. You get fearful. You don't know what to do.
Leader: She is really picking up your uncertainty . . . the fact that you are very unsure about what you're doing. Even when you made that phone call in front of her, you were asking for her approval.

And you are really asking her to go to Phoenix House and find out that it is okay, so that she'll come back and say, "Mama, it's okay. You were really right, Mama, and I love you. I think you really did the right thing, and you're an okay girl."
Gayle: It's more like she's a mother and I'm a child.
Leader: Do you want your daughter to grow up like you?
Gayle: No, I don't.
Leader: You know, being a mother or being a father or a boss is sometimes not so pleasant. Because everybody wants everybody to like us all the time . . . and think we're nice and friendly. After all, the world is so unpleasant most of the time. The last thing we want to lose is the friendship of our kids. And Sylvia knows that, and she uses it. It's blackmail, emotional blackmail, and you are going for it. She knows how frightened you are of losing her affection.

So what if there are times when she hates your guts. Do you remember when your parents laid some unreasonable things on you, and you hated their guts? Well, your daughter is no different. Except that she

is trying to tell you that . . . She started to tell you
. . . That's when you sent her to her room.

(Although Frank and Gayle began to make changes in their life when their son entered Phoenix, they hadn't moved far enough by the time they joined the group to prevent Sylvia from following her brother — first to drugs and then into treatment. Sylvia felt she was shortchanged on affection and credited part of this to the family's all-consuming concern with Steve once his druggism was discovered. This meant that the way to get attention was to use drugs.

Frank and Gayle did get some help from the group. They had started to dig around at the roots of their discord when the sessions ended. By then, Sylvia was already into drugs, and she has since entered the program. Although Steve has noted "great changes" in his parents, and claims, "For the first time, I was able to get down and really rap with them, especially with my father," Frank and Gayle must go much further than this group took them before they reach a permanent resolution.)

11. A Few Final Words

IT MAY BE HARD for parents who have had no rude encounters with drugs to find much in common with our three families. Most couples can coast along carrying a load of discord tucked away. Only when they run up against some gritty reality that can't be bypassed or ignored do their family weaknesses show up. Drugs are such a reality. They can destroy children; they test parents.

Because rampaging drug abuse is a nationwide problem, there are parents who try to shrug off that test, blaming their child's drug troubles on society. But your youngster's drug abuse is *your* problem; protecting your children from harming themselves is your job.

Druggism — the regular use of any psychoactive drug — is a cultural commonplace. It is not a rare or bizarre phenomenon shared by a deviant fraction of the population. The weekend drunk, the chubby wife permanently high on diet pills, and the sleeping-pill dependent down the block are all part of the drug scene. Doctors who prescribe heavily and drug companies that push psychoactive aids for ordinary anxiety reinforce the misguided faith so many Americans seem to have in magical, chemical solutions to human problems.

When your youngster starts thinking about drugs and talking about drugs, he is guided by what he has already seen for himself. You can't be constantly dosing him and dosing yourself with various chemical cures and nostrums without having him pick up the notion that there is a specific remedy for every discomfort. It is an easy step from that notion to an acceptance of drugs that relieve his fears or uncertainties, that help him evade reality.

More important than anything your children learn about drugs are the other attitudes you demonstrate, showing them how you, the adult, manage stress and anger, how you cope with discord or carry responsibility. You must at the same time listen to all the signals that come from them, respond to the noises they make when they are puzzled or hurt or don't understand what is expected of them.

The prolongation of adolescence, the time lag between full physical growth and functional maturity, puts unusual pressures on youngsters and their families. Drugs are a way that some adolescents handle these pressures, a way they cope with insecurity. Drugs offer an escape from *angst,* psychological growing pains, and uncertainty. But the illusion doesn't last; drug-borne security is replaced by more intense anxieties. When drug use becomes a regular part of a young person's life, adolescence itself, the process of change, stops dead, and growth is arrested at that point.

If your youngster tries drugs for himself some day, he will be testing what you have told him or what his peers believe. Most likely you will never learn about his experiments, any more than your parents learned of the cigarettes you filched or the liquor you drank. Most children will experiment and quit. But should they go further, parents must be prepared to do *everything* necessary to stop them. This is not easy. It means using all the muscle you have, making a demand of "no drugs" and enforcing it, refusing to become your children's passive partners in drug abuse. So long as your children are legally, financially, or emotionally dependent upon you, you can make them quit drugs or get the treatment they need. If necessary, you may use the courts to enforce your demand.

While parents have less claim to control over an older child, they often have considerable leverage; for drug users are still immature, and may turn to home for comfort or support. Even a drug-dependent veteran of Vietnam may come to his parents for money or a place to stay.

What we propose in this book often sounds harsh, unnatural, or even cruel. But the job of being a parent makes hard demands, and there are more important stakes than easygoing affection from your offspring. When you come up against drugs, most important is the knowledge that you *can* indeed do something. You can almost always turn your children from druggism. And if you don't, who else will?

Index

Index

Abandonment, fear of, 40–41
Absolute dependence, of a child, 41
Acting out, need for, 31, 52
Addiction: defined, 7–8; progression in, 77–78
Addicts: defined, 6; and crime, 9
Adolescence: surviving dangers of, 52; prolonged, 29–30, 46–47
Adolescent: vulnerability of, 29; choice by, 73
Advertising media, drug pushing by, 22
Aerosol propellant, 7
Affection, need for, 74; between parents, 154
Aggression, adolescent handling of, 52
Alcohol: use of, 59; child's use of, 124
Ambivalence, parental, 57
Amphetamines: misuse of, 10; harmful aspects of, 11; for hyperactive children, 20
Anger: acting out, 31; drug use and, 51; stealing and, 51; parental control of, effect on child, 116
Antagonism, fear of creating, 134
Anxiety: sexual, drugs and, 63; over drug use, 66
Approval, need for, 47, 50
Arguments, parental, 40
Attention, need for, 54
Attitude-forming years, 34

Attitudes, developing, of children, 33; outside influences on, 42
Attitudes, parental, 7, 57, 173; toward drug use, 58, 62, 65

Baby, new, problems with arrival of, 33–36
Bad trips, 12, 70
Barbiturates, overdosage, 12, 124
Behavior: of children, 33–34; assessment of, by parents, 34; of parents, child emulates, 34–35, 39; of mother, effect of, 37; of father, effect of, 39; of divorced parents, 42; of adolescent, 60; at Phoenix House, 88, 90
Behavior control, in hospitals, 20–21
Blackmail, by children, 57, 162
Blacks, drug abuse among, 23–24, 25, 81
Books, influence of, 42
Boredom, contributes to drug usage, 28
Buddy, parent as child's, 40
Case histories: Michael, 77–78; Suzanne, 79; Darryl, 79–80; Dennis, 80–81; Adams family, 101–121; Eddy, 101; Brown family, 122–140; Jill, 123; Cowan family, 141–171; Steve, 142–143; Sylvia, 152
Challenge, by adolescent, 48–49

Index

Children: behavioral attitudes, 33–34; parents confuse, 36
Chipping (heroin), 27
Cocaine, 15, 27
College age, drug use at, 5
Commitment, 83, 131
Common problems, among parents, 99
Communications: maintaining, 43–44; adult-adolescent, 65, 69; among users, 82; between parents, 115–116, 117; parent-child, 123, 143, 149, 170–171
Community responsibility, 3–4
Concern, for Phoenix House residents, 89
Confidence: need for, 25; lack of, 126
Consideration, for spouse, 157–158
Control of child, need for, 139
Courts, assistance by, 71, 124, 131, 139
Credentialism, as contributing cause of drug use, 28–29
Crime, drug use considered as, 18
Criminal activity, 9; to support habit, 28
Cruelty, no need for, 38

Danger in drug use, 3; concern for, 14
Darryl, case history, 79–80
Death, fear of, 40
Demerol, 142
Dennis, case history, 80–81
Dependence, absolute, 41; of adolescent, 47, 48; on peer group, 50–51
Dependency, on drugs, 24
Detoxification, 78, 124
Diagnosing drug use, 13, 67
Diet pills, 19, 79
Discipline: enforcing, 38; breakdown of, 39; lack of, 167
Disciplining, of drug user, 68, 69–72

Dishonesty, parental, 36; problem of, 104
Disrespect, of child for parent, 168–169
Divorce, fear of, 41
Doctors, thoughtless prescribing by, 19
Dominant mother, 139
Dominant spouse, 126–134
Drinking problem: of parent, 106; of child, 124
Dropout, coping with, 50
Druggism: defined, 6; prevalency of, 15–21; fight against, 22; group experience with, 51; treatment of, 82; commonplace condition, 172
Drug laws, problems created by, 18–19
Drugs: suspected use, determining, 13; legitimate use of, 19; dealing with, 53–76
Dumont, Dr. Matthew R., 83

Economy, overdevelopment of, 30
Eddy, case history, 101
Education: at Phoenix House, 87; demand for, 28
Encounters, at Phoenix House, 88–89, 90; of parents, 100; problems emphasized by, 100
Encouragement, need for, 127
Enuresis, 102
Euphoria, 8, 11, 12
Eviction, from home, 75–76
Expectations of behavior, 38

Family, erosion of, 25
Family influence, lessening of, 53
Father: behavior of, 39; ineffectuality of, 139
Father-daughter relationship, 159
Father-son relationship, 160–162
Fighting, between parents, 108, 144, 158, 163
Freud, Anna, 60

Index

Freud, Sigmund, 47
Frustration, adolescent, 30, 31; coping with, 38

Gang, influence of, 26. *See also* Peer group
Ghettos, contribution of, to addiction, 23, 25; dwellers in, vulnerability of, 27
Glue, sniffing, 7
Grandiosity, feelings of, 81
Group encounters, at Phoenix House, 88–89, 90
Guilt feelings, 156

Hallucinogens, 12
Harrison Act (1914), 18
Hashish, 12
Hepatitis, 14, 79, 80
Heroin: psychoactive drug, 5; withdrawing from, 9; marijuana a precursor for, 10; widespread use of, in ghettos, 27; methods of taking, 27; paraphernalia for administering, 28; sexual problems arising from use, 64
Heterosexual relationships, drugs and, 63
Home life, parent's avoidance of, 150
Honesty, in dealing with situations, 43
Hospitals, drug misuse in, 20
Hostility, of parent, 143, 154, 156, 164
Hyperactive children, handling, 33
Hyperactivity, gross, control of, 20
Hypodermic syringe, 17

Identity, problem of, 45–46
Idleness, contribution of, to addiction, 23–24
Illnesses, imaginary, treating, 55
Immaturity: addiction and, 23–24; of parents, 151–152

Impatience, parental, 54
Income, family, lack of, 105, 106–107, 109–110, 125–126, 132
Indecision, 132–133
Independence, physical age of, 46; acceptance of, 48; exploration of, 48–49; demonstrating, 93
Individuality, expressing, 46
Indulgence, by parents, 125
Ineffectual father, 139
Infantile relationships, 110
Information, oversupplying, 43
Inhaling, of drugs, 27
Insecurity, parental, 152–154
Intimacy, drugs enhance, 63; illusion of, 21

Jill, case history, 123
Judgments, necessity for parental, 57
Junior high school, marijuana use in, 27, 80
Juvenile court, aid from, 71, 124, 131, 139

Laudanum, 17
Law, lack of respect for, 61–62
Leisure, contribution of, to addiction, 24
Lennard, Henry L., 19, 81
Liquor, abuse of: by parents, 106; by child, 124
Listening, need for, 49, 161
Loneliness, 75, 81, 82
LSD: increasing use of, 5; euphoria from use of, 12
Lying, 36
Lysergic acid diethylamide. *See* LSD

Mandarin system, 28
Marijuana: psychoactive drug, 7; heroin addiction and, 10; psychedelic, 12; British study of use in India, 15–16; widespread use of,

Index

27; effect of, 59; laws against, 61; rationale for using, 72
Marijuana Tax Act (1937), 18
Maturity: lowered age of, 29; of parents, 107
Mental hospitals, behavior control in, by drugs, 20–21
Mescaline, 12
Methadone, 83
Michael, case history, 77–78
Minorities, vulnerability of, 24
Misuse of drugs: pandemic, 5; drugs commonly misused, 10–11; progressive, 11
Money, abnormal love of, 146, 157, 165. *See also* Income
Money pressures, 103
Moral standards, living up to, 36
Moral values, of children, nonexistent, 31
Morphine, 17
Mother-daughter relationship, 37, 159, 162, 165

Narcotics, abuse of, 23
Needs: of children, as infants, 34; concern for, 40
"No drugs" ultimatum, 68–69, 72
Nonaddicting drugs, 13

Obedience: need for, 75–76; at Phoenix House, 85
Opium, 16–17; in patent medicines, 23
Overdosage, death from, 12
Overindulgence by parents, 161–162

Paranoid psychosis, 11
Paregoric, 17
Parental guidance, 6
Parental responsibility for drug use, 3–14
Parents: confusion among, 31; assessing own behavior, 34; behavior of, emulated by children, 35; insecurity of, 39; needs of, 40; arguments between, 40–41; adolescents challenge, 48; fallibility of, admitting, 65–66. *See also* Case histories
Parents' groups, encounters, 101
Passivity, of parents, 126–127
Peer group, influence of, 26, 169; dependency on, 50; dangers in, 51
Pep pills, misuse of, 10
Peyote, 12
Phoenix Center, 84
Phoenix House, residences, 78; reception at, 83; sites and staff, 84; diagnosing at, 85; internal operation of, 86; resident staff, 86; guidance at, 86–87; routine at, 87; length of stay, 95; special encounters, 99
Phoenix method of treatment, 77–95
Placebos, 13
Police: dereliction of duty by, 26; reaction against, 61–62
Pot. *See* Marijuana
Poverty, as contributing cause of drug use, 30
Preparedness, parents' need for, 4
Prescriptions: dispensing drugs without, 17; for drugs, 19–21
Problems: avoiding, 21; similarity of, in families of drug users, 99; parental, transmittal of, 116
Prolonged adolescence, 29–30; 46–47
Provocation, by adolescents, 49
Psychedelic drugs, 12
Psychiatry and drug abuse, 83
Psychoactive drugs: increase in use of, 5; defined, 7; harm in, determining, 13; avoidance of problems with, 21
Psychological health, defined, 47
Psychopathic inferior, 33
Puberty, 46

Index

Punishment: administering, 38; at Phoenix House, 87
Pushers, 82
Putnam Valley Farm, 77, 84

Racism, as contributing cause of drug use, 30
Reading, influence of, 42
Reality: facing, 55, 104
Reassurance, need for, 48
Rebellion, need for, 47
Relationships: parent-child, 73, 75–76; between parents, 112, 150–151
Respect: between parents, 109, 110–112, 115; for others, lack of, 152; for spouse, 155–159
Responsibility: of adolescent, 47; at Phoenix House, 86, 88; failure to meet, 91–92; parental, 129–130
Rigidity, opposed to ambivalence, 57

School marks, as symptom of drug use, 13, 67, 142
Schools, influence of, 42. See also Junior high school
Security: parental, influence of, 55; need for, 81
Sedation, of oneself, 24
Self-confidence, boosting, 94
Self-expression, adolescent, 49
Self-help groups, 70, 71, 84
Self-importance, need for, 81
Sex, faulty connotation, 147
Sex discussions, parents–peer group, 64
Sexual denial, 152
Sexuality: use of, 37; adolescent, handling of, 52
Sexual maturity, 29
Sexual relationships: providing information about, 43; between parents, 108, 113–114, 115, 117–121
Sexual stimulation, drugs as, 63

Sibling rivalry, 33–36, 43, 103, 107, 143
Snorting, of heroin, 27
Social stresses, 4
Specific encounters, Phoenix House, 90
Speed (amphetamines), misuse of, 10
Status, at Phoenix House, 87
Stealing, 9; and anger, 51
Steve, case history, 142–143
Stress, coping with, 38
Suzanne, case history, 79
Symptoms, of drug use, 13, 67
Synanon, 84

Tardive dyskinesia, 14
Teachers, influence of, 42
Television, drug pushing through, 22
Temper, loss of, 40
Therapeutic communities, 83, 84; treatment at, 72
Tolerance, for a drug, 8
Tranquilizers, 21
Treatment programs, 69; at Phoenix House, 87
Trust, need for, 81

Understanding, need for, 38, 50
Unemployment, as contributing cause of drug use, 23–24
Use of drugs: progressive, 11; diagnosing, 13, 67; excuses for, 65; rationale for, 72; troubles underlying, 74

Veins, marks on, 70, 78
Vietnam war, dissatisfaction with, as contributing cause of drug use, 30
Violence, parental display of, 104, 143
Vulnerability, to drug use, 23–32

Weakness, of parent, 126–134

182 Index

Welfare families, vulnerability of, 26
Withdrawal, fear of, 8–9
Women, middle class, white, drug abuse and, 25

Yelling: between parents, 40; at a child, 131, 148
Youth market, economic factor, 30